Herbs

Herbs

William Denne

LONDON, NEW YORK, MUNICH, MELBOURNE, DELHI

PROJECT EDITOR Emma Callery
PROJECT ART EDITOR Alison Shackleton
SENIOR EDITOR Helen Fewster
MANAGING ART EDITOR Alison Donovan
PICTURE RESEARCH Lucy Claxton, Mel Watson
PRODUCTION EDITOR Kavita Varma
US EDITOR Jenny Siklos

PHOTOGRAPHY Peter Anderson

First American Edition, 2008

Published in the United States by
DK Publishing, 375 Hudson Street
New York, New York 10014

09 10 11   10 9 8 7 6 5 4 3 2

[RD150—March 09]

A catalog record for this book is available from the Library of
Congress Library.

ISBN 978-0-7566-4270-9

Printed and bound by Star Standard Industries Pte. Ltd., Singapore

Important notice
The author and the publishers can accept no liability for any harm,
damage, or illness arising from the use or misuse of the plants
described in this book.

DK books are available at special discounts when purchased in
bulk for sales promotions, premiums, fund-raising, or educational
use. For details, contact: DK Publishing Special Markets,
375 Hudson Street, New York, New York 10014 or
SpecialSales@dk.com.

Discover more at
www.dk.com

Contents

William Denne has gardened with herbs
since childhood and studied at Wye College in
England before joining the RHS Advisory Service
where he became the Principal Horticultural
Advisor at the RHS Garden Wisley. He writes for
the UK's *The Garden* magazine and runs Tasteful
Plants in Kent with his wife, specializing in herbs,
vegetables, and other edibles.

Gardening with herbs

Just as freshly picked herbs in the kitchen add color and excitement to culinary dishes, herb plants have the potential to do the same in the garden. Many herbs have excellent ornamental qualities with the extra sensory advantage of delicious and aromatic foliage. In this chapter you will discover many ways to use herbs in gardens, from the purely productive allotment to mixed plantings, container displays, and formal outlines. Be aware that not all herbs are for culinary use; there are many species that are prized for their medicinal attributes, some of which are highly toxic if misused. Never eat a herb unless you are sure you know what it is, and never attempt to self-administer herbs medicinally without first consulting the advice of your doctor.

The kitchen garden

Orderly rows and serried ranks of vegetables can look very impressive, but leaves valuable spaces vacant. To overcome this dilemma, fill the spaces with a wide range of edible herbs, which need not just be in various shades of green; many can add bright splashes of color throughout the season.

Pictures clockwise from top right

Planting among vegetables Chives (*Allium schoenoprasum*) make a very pretty and effective edging plant, but it is unlikely that a large quantity will be needed as this is a cut-and-come-again herb, which regrows quite quickly. Good-sized clumps can be sown among your other vegetables, perhaps in a grid pattern to help remind you of the crop rotation compartments that are so useful in keeping the plot productive. Planted near peas and beans, chives may also help reduce insect pests.

Crop planning Short rows of lettuce provide the opportunity to grow many different salads and succession sowing can keep crops producing for most of the year. Try interplanting with small rows of leafy herbs, such as lamb's and miner's lettuce, chicory (*Cichorium*), dames rocket (*Hesperis matronalis*), red orache (*Atriplex hortensis* var. *rubra*), and French tarragon (*Artemisia dracunculus*), or perhaps garlic chives (*Allium tuberosum*). If there is the space, grow a large row of comfrey as this makes a superb compost activator and liquid fertilizer.

The community plot The large, dedicated kitchen garden may be a thing of the past, but community plots are very popular again. Many herbs need continual cropping to keep healthy and lush while others just look unattractive when they have been cut or cropped. These are ideal for growing in the vegetable patch, but it is not necessary to grow in rows—clumps and patches can look very attractive. Nasturtiums (*Tropaeolum*) sown in late spring will rapidly germinate and spread into a sizeable clump. Many cultivars are available and they all have edible flowers and the bright colors attract pollinating bees. Try planting them next to your planned salad bed so you can harvest both at the same time.

Herbs in mixed beds

Monocultures can be bland and lifeless, but incorporating herbs into planting schemes bring all the parts to life with each complementing the other.

Pictures clockwise from top left

Mix it up Green roofs planted with low-growing herbs or grasses can be very effective and will help merge garden buildings into other mixed plantings, such as these ornamental grasses, alliums, and *Eucomis*. Structural plants like *Lychnis chalcedonica* also help to meld the two areas.

The allium family Alliums are particularly effective planted where their leaves can be harvested and flowers admired. The same family contains more ornamental forms, such as *A. gigantium* or *A. christophii*, which can be planted between clumps of purple sage (*Salvia officinalis* "Purpurascens"), lifting the planting.

Encouraging insects Planned carefully, the mixed bed becomes a major source of nectar for bees, butterflies, and other beneficial insects. Use a range of plants that flower throughout the summer.

Making a statement Globe artichokes (*Cynara* Scolymus Group) make a wonderful statement with their large flowerheads and silver spiky leaves that contrast vividly with a range of other colors.

Herbs in containers

Medicinal and culinary herbs almost seem to have been designed to grow in containers and the sheer range of pots, troughs, and recycled artefacts that can be successfully used are limited only by your imagination.

Pictures clockwise from top left

Single pot of lavender Lavenders can thrive in pots, especially the slightly more fickle *Lavandula stoechas* and *L. pedunculata* cultivars. The container needs to be at least 12 in (30 cm) deep and wide enough to accommodate the growing plant. Thin metal and plastic pots are easy to handle and can look fantastic in their myriad colors, but offer little protection to roots from freezing weather. Terracotta and wood afford more insulation, but are more prone to water damage.

Contemporary pots Modern pots are very effective and can also be used to simply conceal the plastic pot the herb is growing in. These pots may not have adequate drainage holes, so take care in wet weather or when watering to avoid drowning the plant. In midsummer, temperatures can rise substantially and shiny metallic or plastic pots can heat up sufficiently to cook the roots, so put them where they are not exposed to the midday sun.

Stone troughs These can be very heavy and difficult to position, but they offer the most lovely foil to low-growing creeping or alpine herbs and other plants. Interplant herbs with dwarf bulbs, such as tulips, crocus, iris, and snowdrops (*Galanthus*) for winter and early spring interest. In summer, these shallow containers can be prone to drying out so avoid herbs that are not drought tolerant unless regular irrigation is certain to be done. Troughs often only have a single drainage hole, which can be sufficient to prevent waterlogging as long as they are positioned absolutely level.

Watering-cans Old zinc or galvanized watering-cans spring leaks and become useless for their original purpose, but they make useful planters. As long as it can hold sufficient compost for a herb to grow in over the summer season and without becoming waterlogged, pretty much anything could be appropriated or recycled from the shed or attic, scrubbed up, and planted.

Patterns with herbs

Intricate geometric designs have been associated with aristocratic and monastic herb gardens for hundreds of years, but these patterns do not have to be created on such a grand scale as they can be miniaturized for the modern garden.

Pictures clockwise from opposite

Herb parterre On this scale, herb parterres are inspirational but require high maintenance throughout the year. On a smaller scale, however, their patterns are fun to experiment with and can be incorporated somewhere into most gardens (*see pp.50–53 and 84–85*).

Herbs between railway sleepers Low-growing herbs such as chamomile (*Chamaemelum*) and thyme (*Thymus*) can be squeezed into the smallest of gaps, but it is important to choose your plants with care. Low-growing herbs such as *Thymus serpyllum* or *Chamaemelum nobile* "Treneague" would work here well. Most herbs resent being walked on but the Corsican mint (*Mentha requenii*) is more robust, growing in the tiniest of crevices.

Thymes growing in a wall basket Use wall baskets to great effect to display the different colors and variegations of herbs such as thymes. Hanging a number of baskets together creates an even greater impact. Regular clipping is essential.

Woven herb basket Woven hurdles linked together to form a raised bed provide the framework here for a selection of basils (*Ocimum*) arranged in blocks. Many planting combinations are possible but try to match plants of a similar habit and cropping life so the pattern is maintained. Lawn edgings can also be used, linked or cut into varying lengths so any number of geometric raised beds can be built and filled with your favorite herbs.

Non-culinary herbs

This rich range of herbs may not be edible, but they possess many other garden-worthy qualities beyond being simply beautiful.

Pictures clockwise from top right
Melissa officinalis "Aurea" This perennial herb has a pleasant lemonlike aroma and flavor, but this variety tends to be grown more for its interesting color, compact shape and size, as well as its medicinal attributes. Its cousin, *M. officinalis* (lemon balm), can be a problem in the garden as it is a prolific self-seeder whereas the variegated form is much better behaved. The leaves can be used fresh or dried in an infusion and are renowned for their ability to aid relaxation or even to rejuvenate and alleviate nervous tension or depression.
Echinacea purpurea This herb was the one most widely used in remedies by the North American Indians, many of which have been confirmed by modern research, including its beneficial impact on the immune system. In Europe, it is used in the preparation of over 200 pharmaceutical products, but, as with all medicinal herbs, should not be self-administered without qualified medical supervision.
Hamamelis virginiana The bark of witch hazel is extensively used in medicines to relieve bruises, sore muscles, and inflammation. The shrub is unprepossessing until it flowers in the fall, yielding a soft sweet perfume.
Aloe vera The spiky leaves of this native of southern Africa contain a gel that has remarkable healing properties, soothing burns and promoting regeneration of skin tissue. Unfortunately, it is not hardy and needs a sharply draining soil to thrive.

Other non-culinary herbs

- *Alchemilla mollis*
- *Althaea officinalis*
- *Armeria maritima*
- *Arnica montana*
- *Artemisia abrotanum*
- *Centranthus ruber*
- *Hypericum perforatum*
- *Inula helenium*
- *Jasminum humile*
- *Nepeta cataria*
- *Ruscus aculeatus*
- *Ruta graveolens*

Cautionary herbs

Used extensively in medicine, herbs are invaluable but should only be self-administered under medical supervision.

Take care in cultivation and identification as some cause skin damage if touched and illness, or even death, if swallowed.

Pictures clockwise from top left

Digitalis Foxgloves are grown commercially for their active ingredient, which is used in many coronary or cardiac medicines. There are many species of foxglove growing naturally and in gardens, but all parts of this plant are highly poisonous and if ingested, medical help must be found immediately.

Aconitum Aconites are easy to confuse with delphiniums, but neither should be eaten. The seeds, roots, flowers, and leaves of aconites are highly toxic if swallowed, first stimulating the central nervous system and then paralyzing it—even simple contact with the skin can cause a numbing effect on some people. It is safest not to grow plants such as these where young children can access them or in mixed beds where harvestable herbs or vegetables are grown.

Ruta graveolens This is a small-leaved, somewhat innocuous herb once recommended for inclusion in culinary dishes. It is, however, highly toxic causing mental confusion and inducing abortion in pregnancy. All *Ruta* spp. must be handled with great care as even the slightest contact of the sap with bare skin can result in the skin becoming ultra sensitized to sunlight. The blistering or dermatitis that ensues can be extensive and very painful.

Other cautionary herbs

Be cautious in using or collecting more unusual herbs and be aware that this is not an exhaustive list. Some of those included are only likely to be damaging or poisonous if ingested in large quantities.

- *Acorus calamus*
- *Arnica montana*
- *Artemisia absinthium*
- *Borago officinalis*
- *Hypericum perforatum*
- *Matricaria recutita*
- *Mentha pulegium*
- *Symphytum* spp.
- *Taxus baccata*
- *Teucrium* x *lucidrys*

Getting started

To unlock the hidden talents of your herbs, it is important to think before you plant. A plant growing in the wrong place, or under duress, will never perform well, so get to know herbs and the soil and site you have to offer, before you buy. A little bit of groundwork before you plant can pay huge dividends later, both in the looks of envy from neighbors and friends, as well as in the simple pleasure you will get from having herbs flourishing in your garden.

Know your herbs

Herbs can be very striking visually, but they also possess many other characteristics that may remain hidden unless you get to know your plants' secret talents.

Flavorful herbs Herbs are generally best used freshly gathered. Intensity varies considerably, so only use a little at a time to begin with. Leaves are not the only parts that can be eaten whole or added to dishes as a seasoning. Many flowers have a unique and subtle piquancy while roots and stems are prepared in many inventive ways. Try nasturtium petals in a salad or horseradish sauce, but always remember to only eat herbs that you can positively identify as an edible variety.

- *Artemisia dracunculus*
- *Capsicum*
- *Coriandrum sativum*
- *Foeniculum vulgare*
- *Laurus nobilis*
- *Mentha citrata*
- *Ocimum basilicum*
- *Origanum vulgare*
- *Salvia officinalis*
- *Thymus citriodorus*

Scented herbs Flowers with scent are a great attraction to bees and butterflies, but leaves can also be used, fresh or dried, as a pleasant perfume. The essential oils that produce these aromas are at their most concentrated when the herbs are grown in a hot sunny location and it is worth planting a few favorites in a raised bed or basket so they can be stroked or gathered in passing. Not all herbs are sweet smelling and some can even be used as an insect or cat repellent.

- *Calamintha nepeta*
- *Chamaemelum nobile* 'Treneague'
- *Helichrysum italicum*
- *Hamamelis mollis*
- *Jasminum officinale*
- *Lavandula angustifolia*
- *Lonicera periclymenum*
- *Monarda didyma*
- *Rosmarinus officinalis*

Medicinal herbs Medicinal remedies have been gleaned from herbs for centuries and many pharmaceutical medicines are made from plant sources. Mints, chamomile, and even *Adiantum* (the maidenhair fern) make very pleasant teas from freshly gathered leaves or flowers and can be safely self-administered in moderation. However, many tinctures, infusions, and tisanes of proven benefit in homeopathy and aromatherapy should only be used under the supervision of a qualified herbalist or doctor.

- *Alchemilla mollis*
- *Digitalis purpurea*
- *Echinacea purpurea*
- *Filipendula ulmaria*
- *Melissa officinalis*
- *Murraya koenigii*
- *Salvia sclarea*
- *Tanacetum parthenium*
- *Valeriana officinalis*
- *Viola tricolor*

Assessing your soil

The ground beneath your feet will provide all the nutrients, water, and support that your herbs will need for a healthy productive life, so it is vital that you get to know just how reliable your soil really is.

Different soils

Your yard and gardens will contain a variety of soil types at differing depths. These types fall into a number of textures, which very broadly are silt, sand, and clay. The proportional mixture of soil types, when combined with coarser material and organic matter, tell you how fertile and easy to work your garden soil is going to be. These combinations will also determine how well drained your soil is, which will help you decide when to cultivate your herbs. Soggy soil, for example, is not only much harder to work, but also results in compacted puddles.

As you dig deeper, the soil is likely to gradually change from the top humus or organic-rich layer through a heavier (or perhaps more sandy), compact layer, until you reach a layer in which it would be impossible to grow a herb. It is important not to bring any of this poorer subsoil to the surface as it may impair the fertility and texture of the topsoil, which can vary considerably in thickness, even within the confines of a small garden.

pH test

This important test measures the alkalinity or acidity of your soil on a scale from 1 (acid) to 14 (alkaline) and so helps indicate what types of plant can or can't thrive in your garden. Cheap testing kits are reasonably reliable and readily available with almost instant results if the instructions are closely followed. Try to take a number of samples, as many gardens vary from one end to the other. Remember, too, that most herbs happily grow in the range 5.5 to 7.5 and if your test results are consistently outside this range, it would be well worth seeking a second opinion or engaging some professional advice before attempting to remedy the situation.

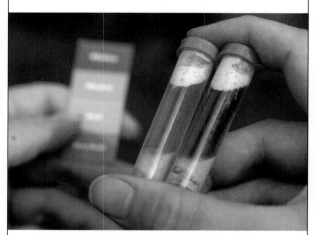

A simple soil testing kit reveals the pH of your soil sample, helping you decide which plants you can grow.

Test your soil

If you are planning a new herb bed or taking on a new patch for the first time, it is important to find out more than just the soil pH. Dig a hole about 8 in (20 cm) square and to a shovel's depth—it is well worth digging at least one hole every 15–30 ft (5–10 m). Pause to inspect the soil you are excavating. If it is dry and dusty, it is likely that you will need to add moisture-retentive organic matter, or if it is sticky or slimy, extra drainage will be a priority. Small stones and gravel shouldn't be a problem as long as there is an equal amount of soil, but large rocks will need to be removed. On new-build or recently renovated sites there may be a thick layer of rubble or clay not far below the surface, which would need to be dug out and removed.

Leave overnight When you have finished digging, leave the holes for 24 hours (cover them with a board to protect from rain or trapping wildlife) and then check for any water in the bottom. If there is only a little water or the hole is mostly dry, nothing needs to be done; but if it is half full or more, the site drainage may need improving. This can be quite an extensive project as it may entail installing pipes or gravel-lined drainage channels to a deep water sump or pond. Your sample hole may fill up with water as you are digging it, which could indicate a high water table and poor drainage. This may just be a temporary or seasonal result, but it does mean the site is not ideal for most herbs, although raised beds may work.

Fill up with water For more information about your soil, fill the hole with water, using either a hose or bucket (pour gently as the sides of the hole can collapse). The speed at which the water drains away will give further indications of the suitability of your ground for herbs and the additives that could be included when cultivating to improve the structure and texture of the soil. More radical drainage solutions may be needed if the water is still sitting there the next day, but this could just be a localized problem—try digging another inspection hole 3 ft (1 m) away and testing again. On very well-drained sites it can be difficult to fill the hole as the water may dissipate as quickly as it is poured in. This need not be a problem, however, as many herbs like this type of soil.

Scrape soil away from sides Once the water has substantially drained away, carefully scrape the sides of the hole with a trowel. The layer most recently in contact with the water will be damp and dark and the extent to which the water has seeped sideways should be clear.

If this horizontal seepage is small, it is possible that the soil is over compacted and simple cultivation may relieve the problem. Additional sand and organic matter added together with rotted compost or manure will also help your soil absorb and store moisture without becoming waterlogged (see pp.26–27).

Improving your soil

Once you have explored the quality of your soil, you may need to improve it. The soil in your garden or community plot is your most valuable resource, but without feeding, the quality of your harvests will deteriorate.

Add organic matter to improve soil structure Organic matter is a vital part of your soil's structure, providing food and nutrients for the essential microorganisms and your crops. Each season that passes and each leaf removed further depletes the soil's resources and ability to produce healthy crops. Moisture is retained in the minute cavities between soil particles, and organic matter improves the water retention for when the plant really needs it. Digging in well-rotted farmyard manure or homemade compost will work wonders for the leafier herbs, but do not apply in bulk to your Mediterranean herb bed as plants such as rosemary and lavender really dislike a moist and nutrient-rich environment.

Add course sand to improve drainage If you have soggy or clay soil, adding course sand will increase the drainage by decreasing the moisture-holding capacity of your soil. This will dramatically improve the range of herbs that you can grow. Incorporate the sand to a shovel's depth and in large quantities. Experiment on a small scale, starting with a depth of 3¼ in (8 cm) over 3 sq ft (1 sq m) before committing to the entire site. Gravel is not expensive, but is very heavy, so calculate how much you need and remember it is easy to add more at a later date. A coarse sand of about ½ in (10 mm) diameter is ideal, but ensure only clean horticultural sand is used as saline contamination can be difficult to remedy.

Double dig to remove a compact layer Double digging is hard work and should not be undertaken lightly, but its effects can last for several years. Mark out the area to be dug (don't be too ambitious) and dig a trench one shovel's depth and two or three wide, carrying the spoil to the far end of the area to be dug in a wheelbarrow. Using a fork, break up the base of the trench to 4–6 in (10–15 cm) and incorporate plenty of sand and organic matter. Dig over a further two or three shovels' widths of fresh topsoil and place on top of the freshly improved lower level, adding more organic matter and sand. Soil from the first trench will fill the last one and any surplus can be scattered over the entire area.

Making your own compost

Everything your garden produces as crop residues, spoiled vegetables, weeds, and prunings can, in theory, be composted and reincorporated into your soil forming part of a virtuous circle of cultivation, production, and recycling.

Composters Choose ready built or made-to-measure composters and ideally they should be big enough to hold all garden waste for at least a year. Space for a composter in a small herb garden can be difficult to find, but if there is only room for a small 3 ft (1 m) square container, it can produce usable compost if fed with the right materials and treated correctly.

Woody and excess material Woody material takes longer to break down, as does dry bracken or straw, but both are valuable additions to the compost bin, helping to aerate the heap. Cut woody stems into pieces the size of a finger and mix in well. Chop up surpluses of any one type of material and store in punctured garbage bags until it can be added in proportion.

Unsuitable material Diseased plants and roots of perennial weeds should not be added as they are likely to reinfect plants or regenerate in subsequent seasons.

Regular turning mixes all the ingredients and increases aeration; water lightly if the ingredients seem dry.

Filling your composter Any organic matter can be added and it will rot if kept moist, so cover the heap with old carpet. Avoid cooked or processed food waste, which will rot quickly but is likely to attract rats and other pests.

Layering In addition, layer green leaves, grass cuttings, vegetable remnants, woody chips, and straw in roughly equal quantities, ensuring that no single component dominates. In smaller composters, add a compost activator.

Growing herbs

Plants can be expensive and identical cultivars difficult to source, but increasing your own stock or growing new varieties is not difficult and is very rewarding in exchange for a small amount of financial outlay.

What do you need?

The bare essentials for raising seedlings include containers, growing media, labels, and the living plant material you are going to grow from. You will also need a watering can with a range of sprinkler heads and a waterproof pen or pencil for labeling.

Buying the full range of pots and plugs can be expensive in one go, but do buy the more robust as they can be reused again and again. Small, frost-resistant terracotta pots are not expensive and are an attractive way of presenting herbs. Organic pots are available, but they are only suitable for one, short-term usage.

Choosing compost A fine sandy texture is good for seeds and cuttings while a coarse grade is better for transplanting older plants. Old compost can harbor pests and diseases.

Using vermiculite This is a mineral that can be added to compost to help alter its air and moisture-holding capacity. It makes the art of growing seeds and seedlings more predictable.

Buying vermiculite Buy a suitable grade of vermiculite, depending on the size of your seed. The coarsest grade can be broken down by rubbing between your fingers.

Seed germination

Seeds that germinate rapidly Seeds that seem to spring up from nowhere need extra care to ensure they have enough space, water, and light. A moment's inattention can result in them becoming cramped and straggly.

- Borage (*Borago*)
- Chives (*Allium*)
- Coriander (*Coriandrum*)
- Dill (*Anethum*)
- Lovage (*Levisticum*)
- Rocket (*Hesperis*)

Seeds that germinate slowly Some take longer, occasionally much longer, so be patient and resist the urge to dig around looking for signs of growth as this disturbance is sure to damage any new sprouts.

- Angelica (*Angelica*)
- Fennel (*Foeniculum*)
- Oregano (*Origanum*)
- Parsley (*Petroselinum*)
- Rosemary (*Rosmarinus*)
- Thyme (*Thymus*)

Chive seedlings emerge quickly and the first leaves are the most fragile—remember that the sun can burn them very easily.

Fennel seedlings emerge after a month or so, but more may pop up a little later—they will soon catch up if there is space.

Common problems

Sowing too much seed Dense sowing results in weak seedlings that are more susceptible to disease and failure. Do not sow thickly unless recommended on the packet.

Mixing up seed To avoid mixed pots of seedlings use fresh compost and only sow one type of seed at a time. Save unfinished packets by folding and sealing with a clip.

Plants quick to bolt Coriander is prone to bolting, missing the leafy stage, if stressed in pots or by too high a temperature. Avoid by sowing directly into the ground in spring.

Growing herbs from seed

The catalogs list many thousands of different seeds and make for stimulating reading—especially over the winter months. Many are easy to grow and it is an inexpensive way of expanding your collection with basic and unusual herbs.

Larger seeds

1 Seed of this size is the easiest to handle. Check the instructions, make sure your palm is dry, and gently scatter at the correct spacing. Use just enough and return the rest to the packet.

2 Planting depth and light requirements vary for each type of herb. Follow the packet's instructions and scatter an appropriate depth of vermiculite over the seeds.

3 Use a waterproof pen to label the pot. It can be useful to record the date of sowing so you can check for germination at the supplier's suggested times.

Dibbing holes

1 For seeds that need to be accurately spaced and at a greater depth, use your fingertips to make indentations in the compost at a suitable depth and distance apart.

2 With big seeds, place one or two in each hole; but with smaller seeds, put in a few more each time. Try not to drop them from high up as they can bounce and be lost.

3 Cover with a 50/50 vermiculite and fine compost mix. Gently firm, label, and water carefully. Place in a warm, light place. Keep barely moist and check regularly for germination.

Fine seeds

1 Lightly dust the seed from your palm or "pinch" a small amount between finger and thumb and carefully sprinkle. Don't sow more seeds than will be happy in a single pot.

2 Finer seeds need a lighter covering of vermiculite using a finer grade and some may need to be left exposed. Be careful watering as too much can flush all the seeds into one corner.

3 Remember to water your seedlings and grow on in a bright place. If the right numbers of seeds are sown in the right container, no pinching will be needed— just transplanting when older.

Sowing plugs

1 Trays come in a range of sizes from four large plugs to many hundreds of small ½ in (1 cm) squares and are ideal for sowing seeds where you only need one or two plants to grow in each module.

2 So you don't lose track of where you are, sow larger seeds on the surface of all the modules and then press them down to the correct depth before covering in one go.

3 Pinch out excess seedlings, leaving the strongest with plenty of space to grow on. Transplant into a larger container or plant out when the plug is well filled with roots.

Growing herbs from cuttings

Many plants do not produce viable seed or, if they do, it is so fiddly or slow to grow that it is easier and quicker to take cuttings from your favorite plant. Always keep your new cuttings moist and in a warm, sunny place.

Softwood cuttings

1 In late summer, select a non-flowering shoot 3–4 in (7.5–10 cm) long from a healthy looking plant. Try to avoid any stems that are too young and soft as these are harder to root.

2 Cut just below a leaf node using clean, sharp snippers and remove the leaves from the bottom half of the cutting. Prepare one cutting at a time so it does not dry out or deteriorate.

3 Insert the cutting 1¼–1¾ in (3–4 cm) deep into a 50/50 vermiculite and fine compost mix. If the cutting bends too easily, it is too young or the compost too coarse. Water well.

Woodier cuttings

Lazy cuttings

1 Select a firm, slightly woody, non-flowering side shoot 2–4 in (5–10 cm) long and gently cut or pull it away from the main stem so a sliver of woody bark remains on the cutting.

2 Trim any wispy strands from the heel and carefully remove all the leaves from the lower half. Insert the cutting into a 50/50 vermiculite and fine compost mix. Water well.

Look carefully at the underside of herbs such as camomile and thyme and you will see aerial roots growing from their stems. These will develop quite happily if detached and grown on in their own plug or pot.

Root cuttings

1 For herbs with invasive roots, such as mint, divide the parent plant into good-sized portions with large fleshy roots for transplanting individually. Do not reuse the old compost.

2 Select a long, healthy, firm root with a diameter of at least ¼ in (5 mm). Look for nodal structures, which appear at intervals and may already be sprouting new roots and shoots.

3 Cut a section 2–2¾ in (5–7 cm) long and with at least one node. Immediately insert vertically into your potting mix. Don't get carried away and grow more than you really need.

Propagating mint suckers

Pinching out

1 Remove suckers from containerized plants as they root if they touch bare soil. Keep one or two for cuttings, but take care where you dispose of the rest as they grow well on the compost heap.

2 Cut just above a leaf node into segments 2¾–4 in (7–10 cm) long and insert four or five into each small pot, so that at least one pair of small young leaves are above the surface.

Sometimes there may not be adequate cutting material available. New side shoots will grow quite quickly if the top 2–4 in (5–10 cm) is pinched out. These shoots might even make good cuttings themselves.

Dividing herbs

Plants are not cheap, and some nurseries are reluctant to divulge the easiest methods of quickly growing more from a single specimen. Wait until your new plants are well rooted before planting out in the garden.

Division by cutting up

1 Many small-leaved, spreading or matt-forming herbs can be easily multiplied by this method, which is best done in late spring or early summer when in active growth.

2 Using sharp scissors, trim excess leafy growth from around the sides and lightly trim the top. This is most easily done with the plant still in its pot. Compost the trimmings.

3 Carefully remove the pot (for washing and reuse) and slice or cut the root ball in half. The bottom part can be discarded and composted as it is likely to be exhausted and root filled.

4 With this herb, the aim is to make plugs with a surface area of about ¾x¾ in (2x2 cm). By carefully cutting using scissors or a sharp knife it is possible to generate nine or ten good plugs.

5 Fill each pot with fine compost, firm down and make a hole with your finger about ¾ in (2 cm) deep. Insert one plug in each hole, gently firm in place, and water well.

6 Label each pot with the plant name and the propagation date. Place in a bright, warm spot and keep moist. Results should be clearly visible within a couple of weeks.

Division with forks

1 Carefully remove the herb from its pot or dig it up from the garden. Gently tease out congested roots and remove excess compost and soil. Passing the clump under a running faucet can help.

2 Gently pull the clump apart with two kitchen forks, detaching sections of the herb, complete with their root systems. Discard any portions that are diseased or damaged.

3 Avoid handling the root system and transplant at the same depth as they were originally. Use containers of fresh, sharply draining compost mixed with vermiculite in equal parts.

Resuscitating leggy plants before division

Teasing apart

1 Leggy plants need not be destroyed as they can be easily rescued to provide many new plants or one compact large one. Partially fill a clean, larger pot with compost and insert the herb.

2 Cover the woody stems with compost up to the base of leaves. Gently firm and keep moist until new roots have developed. The plant can then be divided or its stems used for cuttings.

Many pots of congested herb seedlings, such as basil, parsley, and chives, can be divided. The stems and roots can be very fragile, so break down the clumps into no more than half a dozen portions.

Buying herbs

Shopping for new plants can be very enjoyable, but it is easy to get carried away by the latest, prettiest, most colorful new cultivar or "must have" and spend your budget in an instant. Browsing at flower shows or at nurseries, however, is free and will stimulate many new ideas.

Where to buy

Many people buy their first herb from a supermarket; most likely an intensively produced basil or parsley. At the other extreme is the specialist nursery that stocks many hundreds of cultivars from one or two genera. Happily, in between there are the plant nurseries staffed by knowledgable and enthusiastic professionals, only too happy to help.

Most nurseries try to display their stock when it is looking its best, which can mean in full flower and perhaps not the best time for planting. Ask the staff what would be best and then, as your skills and knowledge grow, you will also feel more at home with the specialists.

What to look for

Space your herb shopping trips over the year as you will soon discover which nursery consistently carries a comprehensive but changing range as well as demonstrating what looks good at different times of the year.

Good points Look for healthy, younger plants whose foliage should be clean, unstained, and free of excessive damage. The compost should be moist but not waterlogged and the surface should be weed free. Clean pots are indicative of young plants grown in an uncongested space. Make sure the labeling is clear.

What to avoid Be wary of buying small plants in big pots as these could have recently being potted up and are not good value. Also avoid plants that look tired, wilted, or have matted roots growing through the drainage holes.

Good versus bad rootballs

Good rootballs A herb should be easy to remove from its pot without damaging the plant or its roots. It will be pest free, just moist and filled with a lose mesh of fine and coarse roots.

Bad rootballs Such herbs are hard to remove from the pot without damaging the plant. It may be waterlogged or have evidence of pests. The roots may be congested.

Avoid leggy plants

Leggy plants These may be cheap, but leggy stems are indicative of overcrowing and poor light. Avoid them unless you have the time and patience to nurse them back to health.

Size of plants

Plugs These are very small plants and are a useful way of growing large numbers of identical plants. Often sold by mail order, they need to grow on before being planted out.

Pot size Price and pot size are closely related, but a large plant can be harder to establish and needs care over periods of drought. Smaller plants may need transplanting.

Large mixed plantings These are a useful way of getting an instantly harvestable selection of herbs. They need regular trimming and dividing or replanting after a season or two.

Harvesting herbs

Fresh herbs and flowers taste so much better when they are gathered from plants grown by your own endeavor—and you know they are free from any additives or artificial preservatives.

Flowers As they are very fragile and crush easily, pick only a few at a time. Collecting into a white container should enable you to discard any unwanted creatures. Only gather flowers from plants in your garden.

Leaves Leaves are at their most flavorsome when fresh, but bunches can be picked for later use. You can use trimmings when pinching out or offcuts when pruning, but remember that over-collecting may weaken the plant.

Seeds Seeds are easy to collect when ripe, but waiting too long results in the birds feeding well. Cut off almost-ripe seedheads and place in a brown paper bag in a warm dry space until fully mature and ready to drop.

Berries Avoid picking berries when they are still wet after rain and only gather a few of them at a time as they can be easily squashed or spoiled. Keep a close eye on their color and ripeness or you will miss the crop entirely.

Roots These can be very messy to gather and it is vital to make sure you are only harvesting the roots from a known herb. Keep some of the identifiable foliage intact when lifting the roots and when washing off the soil.

Herb ideas

Herbs deserve a place in any garden, but if you are a newcomer to this group of plants, it can be good to begin with a bit of inspiration and practical advice. There are several projects in this chapter to get you started, all of which can be put into use in small as well as larger gardens. Remember to maximize your growing space by making use of windowboxes, hanging baskets, and other containers, and plant herbs in unlikely places, such as between patio slabs, where they can thrive.

Making and planting a windowbox

Use containers to bring harvestable crops to your kitchen windowsill. If you can't find the perfect size container, build your own. It need not be expensive or time consuming and needs no special handyman skills.

Tip for success

If you think the wood might split, drill holes using a bit one size smaller than the screw. Partially screw in a number of screws, accurately align, and then screw home in quick succession.

1 Choose a piece of board that is long enough for cutting into two sides, two ends, and a base. Here we used board 6 in (15 cm) wide x 1 in (2.5 cm) deep. Mark out the two sides, two ends, and the base.

2 Double check your measurements—the ends must be the timber width squared (here, 6x6 in (15x15 cm)) and the base 2 in (5 cm) shorter than the sides. To create a neat cut, support both ends of the timber when sawing.

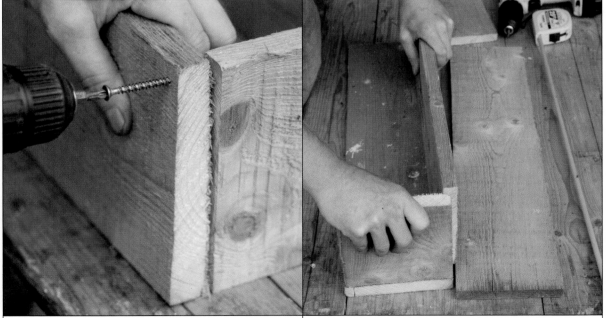

3 Using 2 in (5 cm) self-tapping screws, attach one side piece to an end (two screws should be sufficient), taking care not to mix up the sides and base. If using an electric drill, be careful not to use too high a torque or speed.

4 To ensure the base is the right length, place the box on its side and position the base section on the edge of the side piece. There should be 1 in (2.5 cm) of side showing at the other end. If not, mark with a pencil, cut to fit and realign.

Making and planting a windowbox *continued*

5 Fasten the first side to the other end piece, again with two screws. Turn over, side-face down (as shown here), and attach the remaining side to each end—you may need to gently move the ends so that they line up precisely.

6 Insert the base section into the almost completed planter. Some jiggling may be needed, but if it does not fit, adjust the base as in step 4. Carefully drill and fix the sides to the base with screws at 6–8 in (15–20 cm) spacing.

7 Cut two battens to size to fit your box. These will not be visible, but do need to be about ½ in (12 mm) thick. Invert the box and attach with screws or nails, taking care that they do not protrude into the inside of the windowbox.

8 Good drainage is essential for healthy herbs. With the box still inverted, drill a ½ in (12 mm) hole in the base every 4 in (10 cm) or so, making sure that you don't drill into your work surface.

9 Check that you have sufficient copper anti-slug tape to go all the way around your planter along with a ¾ in (2 cm) overlap. Peel off the adhesive backing in stages and fix to the lower part of the box by gently pressing the tape.

10 For a more permanent slug barrier, nail the tape to the box using ½ in (12 mm) roofing nails at 2–4 in (10–15 cm) intervals making sure that the tape join is securely nailed. This is fiddly so watch your fingers.

11 Fill your planter with a top-quality compost and plant with a range of well-spaced young herbs. Fill gaps with salad leaves like lettuce or chard, taking care to ensure that no foliage creates a bridge over the copper barrier for slugs.

Planting a hanging basket

Edible and aromatic herbs always seem tastier when at eye level and baskets can look spectacular when planted with a range of leaf colors and textures. Hang near the kitchen or barbecue for a readily accessible herb garden.

1 Check that the basket has a good number of drainage holes in the base and sides—a skewer pushed through the liner several times from the outside will help. Partially fill with top-quality fresh compost and gently firm.

2 Carefully remove the plants from their pots and if the roots are congested, gently tease them out a little. Arrange and space out the hardy herbs first, filling larger gaps with tender herbs such as basil.

3 Add more fresh compost around the roots, gently firming down in stages, until the herbs are at the same planting level as in their pots. Trim back any damaged stems or bruised leaves and use later.

4 Water well before hanging your basket and make sure that excess moisture drains away. Select a robust hook and hang carefully as large baskets can be very heavy—especially when wet.

Drying chilies

Harvesting of herbs like chilies can often result in a glut as fall arrives. The stunning colors and flavors can be easily preserved for winter use to spice culinary inventions. A well-cured string will remain usable the following summer.

1 Pick your chilies when they are fully ripe or almost so. Wear gloves if you have sensitive skin and do not touch your face or eyes. Only use fruits that are free of any pest damage or rotting.

2 Using a large sewing or darning needle, thread a strong piece of doubled cotton thread or raffia. Allow about 24 in (60 cm) of string to about 50 peppers and tie a large knot in the free end.

3 Thread your first chili, making sure that the knot is not slipping through the fruit, and then continue to add more. It is best to thread through the stalk, but this can be quite tough, so just beneath it is as good.

4 When your string is full, hang it in a light and airy place until dry. The chilies will lose their bright glossy colors, changing to a glistening rusty-red, but they will not lose any of their flavor.

Creating a parterre

Parterres are ornamental flower, herb or vegetable beds edged by low, tightly clipped evergreen hedges. This herb parterre is ideal outside a kitchen window.

Tip for success

Pinch out the growing tips of the edging plants to produce a compact, bushy hedge. Once established, they can be trimmed three times during the summer to keep them tidy.

1 Clear the site of weeds and then dig in plenty of compost and crushed stone to improve the drainage of the soil. Many herbs originate from Mediterranean-type climates and therefore thrive in such well-drained, dry conditions.

2 When the soil is dry and workable, rake the soil level and remove any large stones or roots of previous plants that might still be in the soil. The best tool for doing this job is a large-headed, stainless steel landscape rake.

3 Tread over the freshly cultivated soil in both directions to firm it and remove any air pockets. Keep your feet close together and firmly press your heels down into the ground. Gently rake over the soil again afterward.

4 Place landscape fabric over the area to be planted. Dig the edges of the material into the soil to help hold it in place. The fabric will reduce the amount of watering and weeding needed later in the year.

Creating a parterre *continued*

5 Measure and mark out the pattern of the hedging with chalk to draw on the landscape fabric and pegs. Keep the pattern simple when designing for a small space, since too much intricacy will look messy and is hard to maintain.

6 With a sharp knife, cut slits into the landscape fabric approximately 8 in (20 cm) apart where the hedging plants are to go. Using a trowel or just your fingers, make planting holes in the soil and firm in the hedging plants.

7 Work around the pattern until all the hedging is planted. The shrubs in this pattern are box (*Buxus sempervirens*), but other suitable plants include *Lavandula angustifolia* and *Teucrium* x *lucidrys*.

8 Arrange the herbs in their pots until you are happy with the design. Larger plants, like this bay tree in a terracotta pot, can be used to create a focal point. Cut the fabric and plant each herb carefully, as in step 6.

9 Carefully check over the herbs and prune out dead growth or shoots and branches that may have been damaged during planting. Brush away any soil or leaves that have fallen onto the fabric and water all the plants in well.

10 Place slate chippings over the surface of the fabric. This gives the parterre an attractive finish and hides the cuts that were made for planting. Other mulching materials can be used instead of slate, such as gravel.

Creating a standard bay tree

Topiarized evergreen herbs can be very expensive to buy, but large specimens do take many years of careful pruning. The techniques involved are simple, however, so try this at home and enjoy spectacular results.

1 Young, single-stemmed specimens are easiest to work with, which can often be bought as pots of young seedlings. Using a healthy, vigorous plant, pinch or cut off enough leaves to create a clear stem of the desired height.

2 To promote bushiness, pinch out all the side shoots to within a few nodes of the main stem. As the branches regrow and fork out, more pinching out will be needed. Remember to save the bay leaf prunings for the kitchen.

3 Pinch out the main growing tip to "stop" the plant from growing much taller for the next year or so. It also helps the other branches fill out. Only pinch out the tip if you are sure that the tree has reached your ideal height.

4 Topiarized bay trees can become quite top heavy and will need extra support. Insert a garden stake into the rootball and loosely tie the stem, in two or three places, to the stake using garden string or expandable ties.

Making a lavender hedge

Attractive to look at and much loved by bees and butterflies, these aromatic features are easy to grow, requiring no feeding and little maintenance beyond an annual clip as the flowers begin to fade.

Tip for success

Young plants need to be firmly planted. Do this by gently pressing soil in toward the roots themselves rather than pressing downward on the rootball.

1 Thoroughly dig over the ground removing large stones and all traces of perennial weeds. Add sand and small stones to heavy soil, but do not add any fertilizer or bulky organic matter unless your soil is very sandy.

2 Dig holes a little larger than the plant pots and, if using larger lavenders such as "Hidcote" or "Munstead," space your plants about 12–15¾ in (30–40 cm) apart. Space smaller varieties 10 in (25 cm) apart.

3 Firm in your plants so the soil is at the same level as the compost. On heavy soil, place the plants ¾ in (2 cm) proud of the soil and add a layer of compost with sand and stones sufficient to just cover the plant's rootball.

4 Water in well immediately after planting and keep moist over their first summer or until established. Try to avoid pouring water over the top of the plant and direct it instead to the surrounding soil at the base.

Making a herb path through a wildflower meadow

Many herbs withstand the odd footstep and thrive in the warmth reflected from pavers. Plant creeping thymes for the best effect; they will soon blur the sharp edges of the paving.

Tip for success

Place gravel around the base of the thymes. Keep this topped up, especially after pruning or trimming, when some gravel always ends up in the soil with the offcuts.

1 After thoroughly digging the ground and incorporating plenty of coarse sand, rake the soil level and remove any roots or large stones. Use long draws of the rake and follow the rough contours of the ground.

2 Firm the ground by repeatedly treading in both directions or use a well-weighted piece of timber. Scrape the timber over the soil to level out any extreme undulations. Do this from side to side and end to end.

3 Measure out enough heavy permeable landscape fabric to cover the length of the path with a 6 in (15 cm) overlap at the sides and ends. Overlap any joints by 6 in (15 cm) and seal together using cloth-backed adhesive tape.

Making a herb path through a wildflower meadow *continued*

4 Permeable landscape fabric is available in packs from 3 ft (1 m) wide to rolls over 18 ft (6 m) wide so, alternatively, you can lay out the fabric and cut it to size. Use sharp scissors to avoid loose fabric strands.

5 Using a spade, push the edge of the fabric into the soil. Some practice might be needed to do this single-handedly and it can help to have two people doing this simultaneously—one on each side of the path.

6 Coarse gravel of ½–¾ in (10–15 mm) size is ideal. Start pouring at one end and work your way up the path in one direction. Don't be tempted to do random sections as this will result in rucks in the fabric that could protrude later.

7 Rake the gravel level, but be careful that the prongs do not catch on the fabric below. Aim for a uniform depth of 1¼–2 in (3–5 cm), but don't worry if this is unattainable as more can easily be added (or removed) later.

8 Create a shallow indentation by lightly dragging a paver across the gravel, then lay the paver into the hollow created. Using gloves, rotate the paver until it is aligned with its neighbors and fill in with gravel if needed.

9 Set out your herbs in their final planting positions and then scrape the gravel away from the fabric surface. Cut an "X" in the fabric, so the edges can then be tucked back or re-positioned to cover part of the rootball.

10 Dig a hole just deep enough to leave the top of the rootball level with the gravel and pavers. Carefully tease out any congested roots, plant, firm gently, and finish off with a final layer of gravel. Water regularly.

Planting recipes

When planting herbs in the garden, you are creating a feast for the eyes, and for the nose and fingers too. Follow these recipes to create your own garden displays, or mix and match the ideas to come up with something to suit your individual situation or tastes.

Key to plant symbols

- ♀   Award-winning plant

Soil preference

- ◌   Well-drained soil
- ◑   Moist soil
- ◆   Wet soil

Preference for sun or shade

- ☼   Full sun
- ◐   Partial or dappled shade
- ☀   Full shade

Hardiness ratings

- ✳✳✳   Fully hardy plants
- ✳✳   Plants that survive outside in mild regions or sheltered sites
- ✳   Plants that need protection from frost over winter

Lavender path

Pathways can seem an extravagance, especially in the smaller garden, but they are a very useful way to showcase a wide range of your favorite herbs. Lavenders and sages (*Salvia*) will gently sprawl over the edges, softening the harsh outline and can even make a straight path appear to be slightly curved. Temporary avenues of single pavers can be placed across borders and intricate patterns of brick or mosaic can be laid in serpentine trails, but all are enhanced when a rotund, aromatic clump of lavender forces you to slow down or change your stride.

Border basics

Size 6x20 ft (2x6 m)
Suits Aromatic, hardy woody herbs
Soil Fertile, sharply drained
Site Sunny and sheltered

Shopping list

- 8 x *Lavandula angustifolia* cultivars
- 7 x *Thymus* "Golden King"

Planting and aftercare

Spacing is of the greatest importance in this type of planting, so before setting out your herbs along the path, double-check the height and spread of each one at maturity. Place the largest plants first and try not to be too regimented— vary the gaps between each plant and consider how tall each will become. Consider the spread carefully as *L. angustifolia* "Royal Purple" can sprawl over 32 in (80 cm), which means that if planted 12 in (30 cm) away from the path edge, it is still likely in time to cover 4 in (10 cm) or more of the path. Regular pruning in late summer as the flowers fade will keep the plants neat and more compact, while a thin gravel mulch applied in spring immediately after weeding will slowly work its way into the soil, helping to maintain the soil structure that lavenders love.

Lavandula angustifolia "Hidcote"
❈❈❈ ◊ ◖ ☼ ♔

Thymus "Golden King"
❈❈❈ ◊ ☼

Lavandula angustifolia "Royal Purple"
❈❈❈ ◊ ◖ ☼

Alternative plant idea

Lavandula x intermedia "Impress Purple"
❈❈❈ ◊ ◖ ☼

Bold and colorful

This dramatic combination is easy to achieve and really demonstrates that herbs do not have to be planted in regimented or orderly patterns to be effective. Try to keep the color scheme simple when creating these types of planting as too many diverse colors will create a kaleidoscope effect. Experiment with different shades of just one or two colors, such as the reddish-purple and green used here.

Border basics

Size 3x3 ft (1x1 m)
Suits Perennial herbs and bulbs
Soil Any fertile, sharply-draining soil
Site A sunny sheltered corner

Shopping list

- 10 x *Allium* "Purple Sensation"
- 1 x *Foeniculum vulgare* "Purpureum"
- 1 x *Lavandula pedunculata*
- 1 x *Salvia officinalis* "Purpurascens"
- 1 x *Alchemilla mollis*
- 1 x *Buxus sempervirens*

Planting and aftercare

Thoroughly cultivate the soil removing all perennial weeds. Position all the woody and herbaceous plants and make sure that they will have enough space to grow —don't forget that the fennel (*Foeniculum*) can grow to over 6 ft (1.8 m) tall. Once these have been planted, put the alliums in between all the other herbs. In the fall, you will be able to buy dry bulbs, but at other times of the year, only containerized bulbs are likely to be available.

Prune and deadhead regularly to keep everything looking its best, but do not remove the foliage of the alliums until it has all died back naturally. The alchemilla may self-seed well, but if the entire plant is cut back hard as the flowers fade, a second flush of fresh green leaves will keep growing until well into fall and winter.

Allium "Purple Sensation"
✽✽✽ ◌ ☀

Foeniculum vulgare "Purpureum"
✽✽✽ ◌ ◗ ☀

Lavandula pendunculata
✽✽ ◌ ☀ ☀ ♆

Salvia officinalis "Purpurascens"
✽✽ ◌ ☀ ♆

Alchemilla mollis
✽✽✽ ◗ ☀ ☀

Buxus sempervirens
✽✽✽ ◌ ☀ ☀ ♆

Birds and the bees

Transforming your garden into a haven for insects and small mammals does not have to mean banks of burrs and overgrown meadows of native species. Herbs are naturally aromatic and many are highly favored by honeybees and other insects. Trees are rarely described as herbs but they add an important habitat and provide much-needed shelter to insects throughout the year. Silver birch (*Betula pendula*) is a great food source for invertebrates as well as thirsty gardeners as the sweet sap can be used fresh or fermented to make a fine wine.

Lavandula stoechas
❄❄◊☼🏆

Rosmarinus officinalis
❄❄◊☼

Border basics

Size 10x10 ft (3x3 m)
Suits A mix of bulbs, perennials, and trees
Soil Fertile, well-drained
Site Any sunny or lightly shaded position

Shopping list

- 3 x *Lavandula stoechas*
- 3 x *Rosmarinus officinalis*
- 15 x *Allium aflatuense*
- 1 x *Betula pendula*

Planting and aftercare

Try to remove all weeds before planting and tie any woody offcuts or stems of dead grass into bundles and hang in a sheltered place to provide a habitat for aphid-munching lacewings and other beneficial insects. Keep deadheading and pruning to a minimum, but remove larger leafier perennials if they collapse after the first frosts. They can cover sections of smaller shrubs that are then liable to be spoiled by the rotting foliage. Leave seedheads for the birds to harvest, but hoe in the spring as self-sown seedlings could take over. Insect pests can be a problem until a natural balance has developed and some damage has to be accepted. Biological controls help, but avoid chemical pesticides, which harm bees unless accurately targeted.

Allium aflatunense
❄❄❄◊☼

Betula pendula
❄❄❄◊💧☼☼🏆

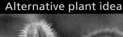
Alternative plant idea

Borago officinalis
❄❄❄◊☼☽

Kitchen potager

Groups of symmetrically arranged raised beds provide an easy and attractive way to cultivate a wide range of herbs without having to set foot on the soil. Keeping the beds small enough so that every part can be reached from the path means that "zero dig" cultivation methods can be tried out as well as allowing for highly intensive mono-cropping of each small section. Different types of mint can be grown for its varying flavors while lovers of chives (*Allium*) will make small work of a single clump. The paths between the wicker-framed raised beds have been kept narrow to maximize growing space and allow easy access. For drama, plant cardoons (*Cynara cardunculus*) and for perfume, add lavender.

Border basics

Size 10x10 ft (3x3 m)
Suits Any type of garden
Soil Good quality multi-purpose or soil-based compost
Site Sheltered site in full sun

Shopping list

- 3 x *Cynara cardunculus*
- 1 x packet seed *Allium schoenoprasum*
- 5 x *Lavandula angustifolia* "Hidcote"
- 1 x packet seed *Coriandrum sativum*
- 5 x *Mentha pulegium*

Planting and aftercare

Sow tender herbs directly into fresh soil outdoors in summer, but for earlier crops, they are best sown in modules indoors from early spring and planted out once frosts have passed. Spaces between permanent perennial or herbs can be in-filled with more sowings of seed sown directly. Toward the end of summer or when light fades, compost any remaining tender herbs, replacing them with parsley and lamb's lettuce sown directly into the soil.

Cynara cardunculus

Allium schoenoprasum
✽✽✽ ◊ ☼

avandula angustifolia "Hidcote"
❋❋❋ ◌ ◗ ☼ ♈

Coriandrum sativum
❋❋❋ ◌ ☼

Mentha pulegium
❋❋❋ ◌ ◗ ☼

Edible flowers

A herb garden at its peak is alive with bees and butterflies busy harvesting pollen from the flowers. Many of these are full of flavor, such as the bright nasturtiums (*Tropaeolum*) that can add a vibrant peppery taste to a salad. They might not look it, but both anchusa and borage belong to the same family and both look good as a garnish for soups and salads or scattered in a fruit cup. For the greatest impact and flavor, pick early in the day and, whenever possible, only select perfect blooms. There are many more edible flower types than shown here, but research carefully before experimenting, as many plants are, of course, poisonous.

Border basics

Size 3x3 ft (1x1 m) or larger
Suits Any style of garden
Soil Fertile and moist but well-drained
Site Full sun or light shade

Shopping list

- 1 x packet seed *Tropaeolum majus* Alaska Series
- 1 x packet seed *Anchusa azurea*
- 1 x packet seed *Borago officinalis*
- 1 x packet seed *Viola tricolor*

Planting and aftercare

All these herbs are easy to grow and can be module sown under cover in late spring and planted out at 4–8 in (10–20 cm) spacings into a weed-free bed once the risk of frosts has passed. Alternatively, sow seed directly into the soil in early summer and thin out once they have grown their first set of true leaves. Regular deadheading and harvesting promote further productive flowering, but reduce the amount of seed produced. Nasturtium seeds are edible when pickled, and can be collected and sown the following year, while borage may freely set seed and regularly re-emerge.

Tropaeolum majus Alaska Series
❄◊◊☀♛

Anchusa azurea
❄❄❄◊◊◊☀♛

Borago officinalis
❄❄❄◊☀◑

Viola tricolor
❄❄❄◊◊◊☀◑

Playing with shape and form

Different shapes abound in the herb garden and there is no one who can tell you what could or shouldn't be planted next to each other. The most delightful combinations often arrive by accident, perhaps from a chance wind-blown seed or survivor from the bird feeder that can then be nurtured or replicated. Shape and form apply to each part of a herb. The curry plant (*Helichrysum*) has silver or gray spiky shaped foliage with flat yellow flowerheads, which contrast with the round-headed alliums, whose long, grass-like leaves are the antithesis to the lemon balm's (*Melissa officinalis*) lush opulent foliage.

Helichrysum spp.
❋❋ ◊ ☼ ♛

Melissa officinalis "Aurea"
❋❋❋ ◊ ☼

Border basics

Size 3x3 ft (1x1 m)
Suits Any informal style of garden
Soil Fertile, well-drained
Site Sheltered pathside, sunny corner

Shopping list

- 1 x *Helichrysum* spp.
- 1 x *Melissa officinalis* "Aurea"
- 1 x *Artemisia abrotanum*
- 1 x *Petroselinum crispum*
- 1 x *Teucrium chamaedrys*
- 3 x *Allium schoenoprasum*

Artemisia abrotanum
❋❋❋ ◊ ☼ ♛

Petroselinum crispum
❋❋❋ ◑ ◊ ☼ ◑

Planting and aftercare

Starting from a clear, weed-free site is easiest, but this form of planting can be fitted in wherever the inspiration or space allows. Don't overcrowd the bed, as this will not allow the shape or form of each component to make its mark. Prune out wayward stems or any herbs that are threatening to encroach on their neighbor and replace any specimens as soon as they detract from the whole. Water well on planting and keep moist until established. Keep a note of times of the year when the planting display gives less satisfaction and consider incorporating bulbs or perhaps a colored gravel or slate mulch.

Teucrium chamaedrys
❋❋❋ ◊ ☼

Allium schoenoprasum
❋❋❋ ◊ ☼

Lower-maintenance informality

Lower-maintenance plantings are the Holy Grail of the gardening world and many herbs do lend themselves to being left alone for much of the year. Large drifts of chives (*Allium*), oreganos, and sages (*Salvia*) studded with the occasional topiarized box (*Buxus*) need little effort to maintain as they are each as vigorous as each other. Framing the entire ensemble by cotton lavender (*Santolina chamaecyparissus*) provides the perfect contrast of silver against vivid green, yet requiring little attention beyond an annual clip. Use the odd pot or container to provide a focal point, and, when little else may be happening, plant up with spring bulbs.

Border basics

Size 15x15 ft (5x5 m)
Suits Hardy perennials and slow-growing shrubs
Soil Fertile, well-drained
Site Sheltered position in full sun

Shopping list

- 10 x *Santolina chamaecyparissus*
- 15 x *Allium schoenoprasum*
- 15 x *Origanum* spp.
- 5 x *Salvia officinalis*
- 3 x *Buxus sempervirens*

Planting and aftercare

Most of the plants used here can be grown from seed, so if time allows, sow sage, chives, and oregano in modules in early to mid-spring. Once the roots have filled their containers, pot them up into 33 oz. pots. Grow on over the summer and they will be large enough to plant out in the fall. Clear the ground of weeds and dig in plenty of course sand. If the soil is poor, add compost or manure. In the first and second year, keep weed free and trim as needed. Each type of plant will need attention just once a year and there should be no bare ground for weeds to enjoy.

Santolina chamaecyparissus
❄❄ ◊ ☼

Allium schoenoprasum
❄❄❄ ◊ ☼

riganum spp.
❀ ❀ ❀ ◊ ☼

Salvia officinalis
❀ ❀ ◊ ☼

Buxus sempervirens
❀ ❀ ❀ ◊ ☼ ☼◑ ♔

Grand designs

Intricate hard landscaping mixed with lush plantings of culinary and medicinal herbs creates an effect that mimics some facets of the great and grandiose gardens from the last few centuries. Ocher-brown or terracotta tiles provide a warm contrast to the cool herbs and hotter plantings of *Artemisia arborescens* and tender purple basil (*Ocimum*), which temporarily fills spaces that will ultimately be filled by its hardier aromatic neighbours. Consider placing seasonally planted containers at strategic points and experiment with shapes as rounder pots can appear more settled when on squarer tiles.

Ocimum basilicum "Dark Opal"
❀ ○ ☼

Aconitum "Bressingham Spire"
❀❀❀ ○ ◐ ☼ ◑ ♉

Border basics

Size 15x10 ft (5x3 m)
Suits Courtyard garden
Soil Fertile but well-drained
Site Sheltered plot with full sun

Shopping list

- 1 x packet seed *Ocimum basilicum* "Dark Opal"
- 3 x *Aconitum* "Bressingham Spire"
- 3 x *Angelica archangelica*
- 9 x *Artemisia arborescens*

Planting and aftercare

Thorough planning and site preparation is essential to make schemes such as this come to life and fulfil their purpose. A plan needs to be drawn to scale and it can be useful to peg out a rough concept on the ground before beginning a detailed plan. You will also need a planting plan detailing the quantities and names of herbs and other trees or shrubs to include. Employ a professional designer for intricate schemes, but you can do much of the soil preparation, herb selection, and planting with their guidance. The shopping list above is for an area of drift planting, such as that to the right of the steps (*see p. 70* for guidance on planting the basil seeds).

Angelica archangelica
❀❀❀ ◐ ☼ ◑

Artemisia arborescens
❀❀❀ ○ ☼ ♉

Alternative plant idea

Buxus sempervirens
❀❀❀ ○ ☼ ◑ ♉

Home remedies

Growing herbs is fundamentally about using them in ways that are natural and beneficial to your health and general wellbeing. The pungently aromatic leaves of *Rosmarinus officinalis* contain essential oils that can be used as a general tonic or mental stimulant. As with all herbal remedies, though, be cautious as although harmless and beneficial to most, it can, in excess, cause pregnant women to abort. Herbal teas are an important part of the magic of "growing your own" and common sage (*Salvia*) and many mints make effective but tasty antiseptic teas, gargles, and mouthwashes. Even innocuous annuals, such as nasturtium (*Tropaeolum*), produce an infusion that helps relieve blocked noses and heavy colds.

Border basics

Size 3x6 ft (1x2 m)
Suits Any informal style of garden
Soil Fertile, well-drained
Site Sheltered position in full sun

Shopping list

- 2 x *Salvia officinalis* "Purpurascens"
- 1 x *Mentha suaveolens* "Variegata"
- 2 x *Rosmarinus officinalis*
- 1 x *Melissa officinalis*
- 5 x plugs *Tropaeolum majus*
- 3 x *Lavandula stoechas*

Planting and aftercare

The backbone of this planting is of woody sub-shrubs, which should be well spaced when planted. Rosemary will take a few of years to fulfil its promise and any gaps can be planted with various cultivars of nasturtium. Sow these *in situ* once all risk of frost has passed or sow one seed to a ¾x¾ in (2x2 cm) module and plant out when the rootball is fully developed. Water in dry weather and deadhead lavender regularly to keep in flower. Let nasturtiums set seed and gather for sowing the following spring.

Salvia officinalis "Purpurascens"
❄❄ ◊ ☼ ♈

Mentha suaveolens "Variegata"
❄❄❄ ◊ ◖ ☼

Rosmarinus officinalis
❄❄ ◊ ☼

Melissa officinalis
❄❄ ◊ ☼

Tropaeolum majus Alaska Series
❄◊ ◖ ☼ ♈

Lavandula stoechas
❄❄ ◊ ☼ ♈

Vertical herb garden

Even if you have a small garden, there is no reason for not growing a range of different herbs in a variety of containers. Using the vertical space reduces the footprint, enabling a greater range to be grown with the added benefit of putting your most aromatic and flavorsome plants where they can be most readily appreciated—without continually bending down. Seek out interesting terracotta containers as the shapes and colors can vary enormously. Not all will be frost resistant, but you can still use them to disguise the black plastic pots of your short-term or annual herbs.

Border basics

Size 6x6 ft (1.8x1.8 m)
Suits Any sunny location with a wall or fence as a background
Soil Multi-purpose compost
Site Full sun

Shopping list

- 1 x *Rosmarinus* Prostratus Group
- 1 x *Salvia officinalis*
- 1 x *Lavandula pinnata*
- 3 x *Ocimum minimum*
- 1 x *Cymbopogon flexuosus*
- 3 x *Ocimum basilicum* var. *purpurascens*

Constructing the supports

Outdoor timber shelving can be bought pre-drilled in kit form and is easy to assemble, or for the rustic-look, use second-hand bricks and weathered planks. Stability is important so check that the back wall is sound. Position two stacks of bricks 4–6 in (10–15 cm) away from the wall and as wide as the strength and length of your planks will allow. Lay one plank on the stacks and add more bricks, an inch closer to the backdrop. As you add the layers, the whole theater will "lean" toward the wall with little risk of toppling over. For added stability, add shelf brackets.

Rosmarinus Prostratus Group
❄❄ ◌ ☼ ♈

Salvia officinalis
❄❄ ◌ ☼

Lavandula pinnata
❄◌ ☼

Ocimum minimum
❄◌ ☼

Cymbopogon flexuosus
❄◌ ☼

Ocimum basilicum var. *purpurascens*
❄◌ ☼

Informal formality

Well-tended box hedges (*Buxus*) can seem very precise and formal, but the rigid lines can be softened to create an image of structured relaxation and calm. Allowing the odd box plant to grow taller and bushier enables some experimentation in topiary or clipping to shape. Blocks of solid planting mellow when more than one cultivar of the same genera are mixed, as with these various *Lavandula angustifolia*, planted to contrast with the *Alchemilla mollis* in the background, which is allowed to sprawl unchecked over the paths. Box hedges frame the upright flowering spikes of foxglove (*Digitalis purpurea*). Don't forget the vertical aspect as this can draw the eye toward the core of the vista. In this stunning array, *Foeniculum vulgare* "Purpureum" acts as a soft central spindle to the herbal planting.

Border basics

Size 15x15 ft (5x5 m)
Suits Larger gardens
Soil Fertile, moist, but well-drained
Site Border in full sun

Shopping list

- 5 x *Digitalis purpurea*
- 5 x *Alchemilla mollis*
- 10 x two cultivars of *Lavandula angustifolia*
- 1 x *Foeniculum vulgare* "Purpureum"
- 50 x *Buxus sempervirens*

Planting and aftercare

Complicated plantings demand thorough soil preparation including weed removal and incorporation of plenty of gravel and well-rotted compost or manure in equal quantities. Plant in stages, doing the box first, in the fall. Aftercare is intensive, as the diversity of herbs used need deadheading, clipping, or cutting back at differing times. Biennials, like the foxgloves, need replacing every other year unless allowed to set seed.

Digitalis purpurea
❀❀❀ ◊ ☼ ☼

Alchemilla mollis
❀❀❀ ◊ ☼ ☼

Lavandula angustifolia
❀❀❀ ◊ ◊ ☼

Foeniculum vulgare "Purpureum"
❀❀❀ ◊ ◊ ☼

Buxus sempervirens
❀❀❀ ◊ ☼ ☼ ♛

Culinary planting

A sheltered sunny space just by the kitchen door or on the patio next to the barbecue is ideal for a couple of planters containing all the herbs you regularly use. Intersperse the ordinary culinary herbs, such as mint and thyme, with a few other more esoteric or seasonal varieties, like basils (*Ocimum*) or garlic chives (*Allium sativum*). Also try the more colorful sage, *Salvia officinalis* "Icterina," which has oodles of flavor combined with a striking appearance. Treat this planting as a temporary buffet that can be harvested as often as needed, or as a plot where you can trial new finds before planting out in your main borders or herb garden.

Container basics

Size 18x18 in (45x45 cm)
Suits Any style of garden
Soil Multi-purpose compost with added coarse sand
Site Full sun by kitchen door

Shopping list

- 1 x *Salvia officinalis* "Icterina"
- 1 x *Mentha* "English Garden"
- 1 x *Petroselinum crispum*
- 1 x *Origanum vulgare* "Aureum"
- 1 x *Foeniculum vulgare* "Purpureum"

Planting and aftercare

Fill your containers with multi-purpose compost mixed with approximately 20 percent coarse sand. Make sure the drainage holes are clear of the ground using pot feet or supports to aid drainage. Position your plants so the trailing herbs are on the edge and taller plants, such as the fennel (*Foeniculum*), are in the center. Water in well and keep moist in summer. Lghtly trim or pinch out the tips regularly. Replace tired plants by digging out the rootball with a couple of handfuls of old compost. Replant with fresh transplants, filling in with fresh compost as needed.

Salvia officinalis "Icterina"
❄❄ ◊ ☼ ♈

Mentha "English Garden"
❄❄❄ ◊ ◐ ☼

Petroselinum crispum
❄❄❄ ◊ ◊ ☼ ☀

Origanum vulgare "Aureum"
❄❄❄ ◊ ☼ ♜

Feoniculum vulgare "Purpureum"
❄❄❄ ◊ ◊ ☼

Mediterranean magic

In a warm, sheltered corner of the garden, drought-tolerant herbs can be easily combined to recreate the scent and impact of a modern Mediterranean courtyard in miniature. Choose plants that will form well-defined clumps, such as *Salvia officinalis* "Purpurascens" and *Origanum vulgare* "Aureum" intertwined with the lower spreading *Thymus serpyllum* cultivars. Allow some of the more relaxed herbs, such as *Rosmarinus* Prostratus Group, to gently work their way down the white walls where their fine foliage will be sharply defined and the flowers of *Achillea millefolium* (planted at the base of the wall) will be perfectly silhouetted.

Border basics

Size 10x10 ft (3x3 m)
Suits Drought-tolerant Mediterranean herbs
Soil Fertile, sharply-draining
Site Full sun and sheltered from wind

Shopping list

- 3 x *Salvia officinalis* "Purpurascens"
- 5 x *Thymus* spp.
- 1 x *Achillea millefolium*

Planting and aftercare

Good drainage is essential for Mediterranean herbs, so dig over the soil well and incorporate plenty of coarse sand. Plant in fall or spring, avoiding a hot sunny day, and water in well. More gravel applied as a mulch will help maintain moisture during the hottest, driest periods of summer and keep the foliage free of dirty marks that are caused by soil splash.

As many of these herbs are planted at eye level, deadhead regularly and remove faded or damaged foliage. In late fall or early winter, cut back the herbaceous foliage and give the more woody herbs a light trim.

Salvia officinalis "Purpurascens"
❄❄ ◊ ☼ ♆

Thymus pseudolanguinosus
❄❄❄ ◊ ☼

chillea fillipendulina
❄❄❄ ◊ ◊ ☼

Thymus "Golden King"
❄❄❄ ◊ ☼

Alternative plant idea

Rosmarinus officinalis
❄❄ ◊ ☼

Hot peppers

Even the blandest of foods can be spiced up with the addition of fresh chili pepper. For the quickest results, small fruiting plants can be bought from nurseries or specialist growers, but they are also easy to grow from the wide variety of seeds available. Look for the long, thin "Pinocchio's Nose," which can reach 12 in (30 cm) long and turns red when ripe, or the stubbier "Hungarian Hot Wax;" but remember, color and size is no indicator of hotness. Take care when handling the fruits and seeds and wash your hands, as inadvertently rubbing your eyes can be very painful.

Container basics

Size 8x8 in (20x20 cm) pot per plant
Suits Any style of garden
Soil Rich multi-purpose compost
Site Greenhouse, conservatory, or sheltered windowsill in full sun

Shopping list

- 1 x chili pepper "Golden Cayenne"
- 1 x chili pepper "Pinocchio's Nose"
- 1 x chili pepper "Fillius Blue"
- 1 x chili pepper "Hungarian Hot Wax"
- 1 x chili pepper "Prairie Fire"
- 1 x chili pepper "Cayenne"

Planting and aftercare

Sow seed according to packet at a temperature of 68–77°F (20–25°C) in a 50/50 mix of vermiculite and multi-purpose compost. Sow one or two seeds per small pot and lightly cover them with a sprinkling of vermiculite. Keep moist using tepid water and do not over water. Germination can be in 10–14 days, but may take considerably longer. Transplant when the roots have filled the existing container—chilies do like to be tight in their pots. When the flowers begin to form, start feeding the chilies with a liquid fertilizer and keep in a warm spot. Over winter for an even better crop in the second year.

Chili pepper "Golden Cayenne"
❄◊ ☼

Chili pepper "Pinocchio's Nose"
❄◊ ☼

Chili pepper "Fillius Blue"
❄◊ ☼

Chili pepper "Hungarian Hot Wax"
❄◊ ☼

Chili pepper "Prairie Fire"
❄◊ ☼

Chili pepper "Cayenne"
❄◊ ☼

Hanging herb and vegetable basket

Vegetable gardening does not get much more convenient than picking juicy cherry tomatoes and fragrant herbs from just outside your back door. Hanging baskets are often associated with bedding plants, but why not try planting a combination of cascading cherry tomatoes, vibrant nasturtiums (*Tropaeolum*), and delicious herbs instead? Kept fertilized and watered and they will look great over a long season and provide tasty, fresh produce for the kitchen as well.

Container basics

Size Basket at least 25 cm (10 in) in diameter
Suits Area close to the kitchen
Soil Multi-purpose potting mix
Site Wall in full sun and sheltered from strong winds

Shopping list

- 1 x *Mentha* "Chocolate Peppermint"
- 1 x *Petroselinum crispum*
- 1 x *Thymus citriodorus* "Golden Lemon"
- 1 x tomato "Tumbler"
- 1 x *Allium schoenoprasum*
- 1 x *Tropaeolum majus* Alaska Series

Planting and aftercare

Ensure that drainage holes have been made in the base of the basket. Place a layer of lightweight potting mix in the bottom, then position the plants, still in their pots, to see where they will look best. Remember that trailing plants should be near the edge of the container. Once you have settled on a design, water the plants well, remove them from their pots, and place in the basket. Fill the gaps with potting mix, firming around the plants, and water the basket thoroughly. Hang it on a sturdy hook and water regularly. Once the tomatoes begin to set, apply a liquid tomato fertilizer weekly.

Mentha "Chocolate Peppermint"
✽✽✽ ◊ ◑ ☼

Petroselinum crispum
✽✽✽ ◊ ◑ ☼ ☀

Thymus citriodorus "Golden Lemon"
✽✽✽ ◊ ☼

Tomato "Tumbler"
✽◊ ◑ ☼

Allium schoenoprasum
✽✽✽ ◊ ☼

Tropaeolum majus Alaska Series
✽◊ ◑ ☼ 🏆

Taking care of your herbs

It is satisfying to know that herbs are among the easiest edible plants to grow and take care of. Just by harvesting them you are helping to maintain them, as many—such as rosemary and thyme—seem to thrive on such regular attention, which keeps them tidy, compact, and prolific. A little watering and feeding from time to time will keep them in tip-top condition, particularly if they are growing in pots, and remember to pinch out, weed, and remove untidy seedheads and foliage to keep them looking their very best.

Feeding herbs

All plants need sustenance to keep them healthy and herbs are no different. Soil and potting compost tire quickly and regularly need replenishing or feeding.

Nutrient deficiency The signs of nutrient deficiency are typically a reduction in general vitality sometimes combined with a yellowing or reddish-brown mottling of the leaves. These symptoms can easily be confused with wind scorch, drought, or water logging and it would be a mistake to reach for the fertilizer or mineral supplements without first checking for these disorders. Dig a small hole under the canopy of larger herbs or next to the rootball, if newly planted, and feel how wet the soil is (*see p.97*).

Types of fertilizer

Finding the right type of fertilizer can be bewildering when faced with the range of ready-mixed liquid, granular, or slow or rapid release fertilizers, none of which are really a substitute for digging in compost or farmyard manure. Ask for advice and remember that different plants tend to need different formulations. Regular transplanting will minimize the amount of extra feeding needed and this can be supplemented by using foliar applications. A scattering of general-purpose, balanced fertilizer will keep most of your plants quite content.

Add granular formulations to the soil surface or mix with compost when transplanting—follow the manufacturer's recommendations.

Liquid fertilizers come in powder or concentrated liquid form; use a dedicated watering can to avoid mix-ups with weedkillers.

Watering herbs

Watering The amount and frequency of watering that your herbs require will vary depending on climate and season, but all are likely to need extra moisture when recently planted and when in active growth. Try to apply the water directly but gently to the soil or mulch rather than soaking the leafy canopy as this can cause damage and promote fungal diseases.

Containerized herbs are likely to need daily watering, especially in hot weather, but some, such as basil, will resent going to bed at night with wet leaves or waterlogged compost, so water in the morning before they are in direct sunlight.

In winter, watering probably won't be needed, but continue to check your herbs for signs of waterlogging and even drought as plants can rapidly dry out in cold windy weather. Don't forget your over-wintering, tender herbs and spring seedlings in the conservatory or greenhouse, but avoid using water straight from the water butt or tap on these as the sudden cold can shock them to a standstill.

Is watering necessary? The surface layer of a pot often looks dry or is covered with a gravel mulch. Pushing a finger through into the compost gives a good indication of how wet or dry the compost really is. Lifting the pot and gauging its weight also gives an accurate indication.

Help yourself Mulches are available in a wide range of natural and recycled materials and help reduce evaporation from the soil. This can mean less watering, but also makes watering harder to gauge. Take extra care in winter and wet weather to keep the compost just moist.

Pruning and trimming

Herbs respond well to regular attention and can become lank and woody or sprawl untidily unless they are cut back or deadheaded each year.

Cutting back after flowering Pruning out of finished or fading blooms can help promote the development of further bursts of flower buds, but not all herbs are capable of flowering continuously. Some, such as *Lavandula angustifolia*, will only flower once, but others, such as cultivars of *L. stoechas* and *L. pinnata*, can flower almost continuously throughout summer if the flowering stem is cut back to a node or to lower developing buds.

Herbs such as lemon balm (*Melissa officinalis*) and fennel (*Foeniculum*) will seed themselves prodigiously if not deadheaded or cut back. Deadheading will also prevent seed development, so always leave a few to set if you wish to harvest the seed for sowing or culinary purposes.

Trimming back

Maintaining a neat and productive set of culinary herbs is dependent on regular usage or harvest. New growth is the most colorful and flavorsome and to keep this coming, regular rejuvenation is vital. Trimming off flowerheads will often prevent annuals and biennials from dying while perennials may go on to produce a second flush of foliage.

As the flowers fade, cut back with sharp scissors, aiming to reduce the stems by about half on the first occasion.

The foliage will grow back by ½–¾ in (1–2 cm) within a few weeks and this new growth can be trimmed off for immediate use.

Hard pruning

Many herbs are shrubs and some, such as santolinas and *Helichrysum italicum* (pictured here), can become woody and sparse at their bases. Renovate in late spring or early summer when there is little chance of the tender new growth being damaged by frosts. Some of the prunings could even be used as cutting material.

Using sharp pruners, cut out all dead and diseased wood to just above ground level; cut back all other stems to around 4 in (10 cm).

Thin out the remaining branches to leave 6–12 stems with a number of new shoots on each—aim for an open goblet shape.

Shearing lavender

Hedges of *Lavandula angustifolia* and its cultivars need pruning at least once a year to keep them compact and robust. An additional light trim in early spring delays flowering by a few weeks but helps keep the hedge in good shape. Never prune into old wood as it is unlikely to regenerate and may also cause rots to develop.

In late summer or as the flowers begin to fade, cut back most of the previous season's growth using sharp shears or pruners.

Aim to leave ¾–2 in (2–5 cm) of actively growing or budding wood and make sure no lose trimmings are left to rot in the hedge.

Maintaining your herbs

Herbs are generally quite robust plants but do appreciate a little bit of attention now and then. Leaving them to do their own thing is tempting, but many can get carried away if untended and spread themselves everywhere.

Spread out the workload Throughout the gardening year there is always something that can be usefully done, but in spring and fall there rarely seem to be enough hours in the day, so get as much done in the winter as you can. Try to plan your new schemes in the fall so the hard digging can be done on dryer days in early winter and the soil can be ready for planting in the spring. Pruning and cutting back do not have to be done in the fall—left standing, stems and seedheads provide a habitat and food source for wildlife. In summer, much of the harvesting, pruning, and pinching out is best done in small doses—it makes the process more enjoyable.

Pinching out By pinching out the growing tips of herbs such as basil (*Ocimum*), the plant bushes out as its energy is redirected to lateral buds lower down the stem. Avoid the temptation to just pick off the odd leaf.

Weeding This is essential to reduce competition for light, water, and nutrients, but take care not to damage your herbs by over-enthusiastic hoeing. This can be an easy task if done regularly, but onerous if left too long.

Removing seedheads Do this as the seeds ripen if you want to harvest them or prevent wanton self-seeding. Remember, though, that some can look good in winter and are also a useful food source for the birds.

Rampant herbs

Armoracia rusticana Horseradish is a large, vigorous plant whose tasty roots can taper down over 60cm (24in) into the soil and can be very difficult to dig out. It will spread quite rapidly and if you really do want to grow this plant, it would be a good idea to give it its own raised bed within which it can be contained. It will need to be fed extra compost or manure as it requires a fertile soil to produce a good crop and really won't be productive in a pot.

Removal of the herb, if it has taken over, is arduous and it is important to remove every fragment of root from the soil, as each piece is capable of regenerating and growing to full size within a season or two.

Melissa officinalis and alliums Lemon balm can set seed prodigiously and in time it springs up in every crack or crevice. The flowers are small and insignificant, which can make it difficult to know when to deadhead. An easier method is to cut the whole plant down to within 6 in (15 cm) of ground level as soon as it is 20–24 in (50–60 cm) tall. Alternatively, plant its cousin *Melissa officinalis* "Aurea," which is more compact and seems to be a bit better behaved.

Alliums can also become a problem as they copiously set seed as well. The seedlings appear in spring but are easy to gather and use as baby chives. Alternatively, hoe them off before they become established.

Mints (*Mentha* spp.) These are renowned for rapidly spreading and invading ground where they are not wanted, quickly forming a mass of intertwining stems, roots, and suckers. Avoid this by planting in a container, but do make sure that the drainage holes are blocked with landscape or weed-control fabric as mint will find and exploit any avenues to escape. Bury or sink containers in the ground to just below the rim, but keep a watchful eye as laterally spreading suckers or runners will soon extend beyond the edge and will root very rapidly. Despite this, mints are an essential herb, but do try to avoid planting several types of mint per container as one will become dominant and overpower the rest.

Keeping pests at bay

The biodiversity in your yard and garden will contribute to the pleasure you gain from growing herbs, but some wildlife will be beneficial, while others may appear to be incurable pests.

Friendly insects Beneficial insects come in many shapes and sizes, but their numbers can be curtailed by misguided pesticide applications or as a result of inaccurate identification. Many are essential pollinators while others are predators feeding on plant pests and other invertebrate animals. These include ladybugs, some hoverfly larvae, and lacewing larvae, while ground beetles feed on a wide range of soil-dwelling pests.

Biological control This is the use of nature's own armory of predators, parasites, and pathogens to control pests. They are of most use where they can be released into a protected environment, such as a greenhouse. Some nematodes, as used to control slugs and vine weevil, can also be used outdoors, but only when soil temperatures are at or above 41°F. Accurate and early identification is essential to ensure the correct control is used and at the right time of year. If in any doubt, seek advice. In some cases, chemical control may be the only option when you have an infestation, but only apply according to the instructions, especially when spraying edible crops. Be aware that the use of insecticides is likely to kill biological controls and beneficial insects.

Barriers Barriers are a very useful way of preventing pests from getting to your prized herbs, let alone damaging them. Most are designed to counteract the pest by being uncomfortable to cross or impossible to jump or climb over. Copper tape supposedly gives slugs a small but harmless electric shock, while bands of vaseline or grease make movement difficult for slimy creatures. Take care to remove fallen vegetation as this can create a bridge that will soon be discovered and exploited to the full. Sharp sands, gravels, and ground-up eggshells are used relatively successfully to restrict snail damage. Used on their own, each provides a modicum of protection, but if used in conjunction with biological control and considered use of slug pellets, any damage will be minimal.

Common pests

Slugs and snails These cause massive damage to seedlings and developing leaves. Organic control can be hopeless, but reducing the population using pet-friendly pellets from early spring may enable less drastic methods to be used in future.

Vine weevils Adults leave notches in leaf margins and larvae devour roots. Use insecticidal drenches on non-edible container plants, but biological controls are also available. The adults are active at night when they can be seen by flashlight and destroyed.

Aphids Watch for signs of a growing infestation, including ants rushing around or stems and leaves sticky with honeydew. Biological and chemical controls are available and can be effective, but the former is best reserved for indoor crops.

Bay sucker nymphs These insects suck sap, causing leaf curling and discoloration. As adults they may be visible, resting on young shoot tips, and should be picked off. Insecticides are unlikely to be effective, but removing affected leaves can help.

Rosemary beetles They look beautiful, but are a serious pest of lavender and rosemary. Control by removing adults and larvae by hand, or spray ornamental plants with insecticides and treat culinary herbs with pyrethrum or thiacloprid.

Rabbits and hares Such pests can cause severe damage and may even kill young trees and other plants. Tree guards or fencing can be effective, but keep a close watch for gaps. Live trapping can also be used where fencing is not practical.

Common problems

Diseases and other problems are an inevitable part of gardening, but a few simple measures can significantly reduce the number that occur as well as their impact. Some will still get through and accurate identification is vital for the right solution to be used.

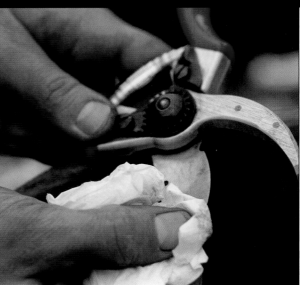

Pruners These and other tools are used throughout the garden and can carry fungal and bacterial infections from one plant to the next. Try to clean the blades of your pruners at the end of each day using a cloth soaked in domestic disinfectant. When pruning diseased material, wipe the blades before moving on to the next plant.

Contented plants Strong plants are less susceptible to infection. Ensure your herbs have plenty of air and space to grow on without exhausting their water or nutrient supplies and provide shade if the sunlight is too strong. Remove infected or severely damaged plants immediately. Burn diseased material and do not reuse spent compost.

Spraying This need not just include synthetic pesticides, which could be harmful to wildlife. Careful use of foliar feeds and preventative natural extracts can be helpful. If using a licensed chemical product, identify the pest before application following the manufacturer's instructions—your herbs are, on the whole, an edible crop.

Identifying common problems

Powdery mildew This disease is exacerbated by dry soil and humid air. Infected leaves may become yellow and distorted. Control by removing infected material and reducing overhead irrigation. On non-edible crops, use a licensed fungicidal spray.

Mint rust Most commonly seen on mint, small orange-brown fungal spore pustules occur on the stems and leaf undersides, sometimes accompanied by leaf distortion in the spring. Destroy infected plants and do not reuse the potting compost.

Curling leaves This does not always indicate a pest or disease. Natural and synthetic pesticides and herbicides can cause damage, even in very small doses. Sprayed green waste can be composted but it is only reliably safe to use after a number of years.

Damping off This occurs to young seedlings and can look like wilting. The cause is a fungal infection that thrives in damp, airless, low-light conditions. Prevent it happening by only using clean materials and germinate seeds in light, airy conditions at the correct temperature.

Ants Ants are not really a problem in the herb garden, but they can be an irritant. They are, however, a useful indicator as they scurry over the stems of plants where an aphid colony is developing. The ants "farm" the aphid honeydew and protect them from other predators.

Over watering Too much rain, irrigation, or poor drainage will severely damage and even kill many herbs, but it is easy to mistake the superficial symptoms for drought. Inspect the root system to determine which is the problem. Some plants will recover with repotting.

Plant guide

No garden is complete without at least a small selection of herbs, even if you limit yourself to just the basic essentials like mint, basil, thyme, and rosemary. Beyond the kitchen, herbs also make excellent garden plants. Many are statuesque, like feathery fennel, while others are evergreen and so make effective structural plants.

Key to plant symbols

⚆   **Award-winning plant**

Soil preference

◊   **Well-drained soil**

◖   **Moist soil**

●   **Wet soil**

Preference for sun or shade

☼   **Full sun**

☼   **Partial or dappled shade**

☀   **Full shade**

Hardiness ratings

❋❋❋   **Fully hardy plants**

❋❋   **Plants that survive outside in mild regions or sheltered sites**

❋   **Plants that need protection from frost over winter**

❀   **Tender plants that do not tolerate any degree of frost**

Plant guide (Ac–Al)

Achillea ageratum
Also known as English mace, this aromatic perennial will grow almost anywhere, in any type of soil and looks statuesque in a large terracotta pot. Young tender leaves are best used in soups and for flavoring rice and pasta.

H: 24–28 in (60–70 cm); **S**: 24–28 in (60–70 cm) ❋❋❋ ◊ ◖ ☼

Achillea filipendulina
A very large, rumbustious plant, grow it where there is plenty of space. The flowers are very attractive to beneficial insects, but should be deadheaded as they fade to prevent self-seeding—other trimmings make a useful compost accelerant.

H: 4 ft (1.2 m); **S**: 18 in (45 cm) ❋❋❋ ◊ ◖ ☼

Achillea millefolium
Literally translated as "a thousand leaf," this daintily foliaged cultivar will form a good clump over time. Useful in coastal regions, *Achillea* can be invasive if left to its own devices. Small amounts of young aromatic leaves are good in salads.

H: 24 in (60 cm); **S**: 24 in (60 cm) ❋❋❋ ◊ ◖ ☼

Acinos alpinus
Basil thyme is a fully hardy perennial that is short lived and often fails to deliver its minty thymish scent. Best grown as an annual, it is no longer much used as a culinary or medicinal herb, but use the most aromatic flowering plants in salads.

H: 4–8 in (10–20 cm); **S**: 3–6 in (8–16 cm) ❋❋❋ ◊ ☼

Aconitum napellus
Monkshood (or wolfsbane) is a stunning plant for most soils and thrives in dappled shade. Despite being very poisonous, it is extensively used in the pharmaceutical industry. If planting, site well out of reach of young children and grazing livestock.

H: 5 ft (1.5 m); **S**: 12 in (30 cm) ❋❋❋ ◊ ◖ ☼ ☼

Acorus calamus
Useful in wet soil or shallow water, sweet flag can provide structure to marginal plantings. Used in the past to produce an antibiotic tranquillizing oil, but its use is declared unsafe as a medicine in many parts of the world, including the US and UK.

H: 24–36 in (60–90 cm); **S**: 24 in (60 cm) ❋❋❋ ◖ ◖ ☼

Acorus gramineus
Japanese rush is a semi-evergreen perennial that can be freely planted in aquariums, shallow water, and bog gardens and the rhizomes harvested (when not in flower) for roasting or stir-frying. Replant unused rhizomes to ensure continuity of supply.

H: 3–14 in (8–35 cm); **S**: 24 in (60 cm)
❀◐●☀

Adiantum capillus-veneris
The maidenhair fern is a medicinal herb that is easy to grow in shady sites as long as it is not allowed to dry out. Its leaves also make a refreshing tea. It spreads readily without being invasive and is easy to propagate in spring by division.

H: 12 in (30 cm); **S**: 16 in (40 cm)
❀❀◐☀

Aegopodium podagraria
Ground elder is definitely not a herb to deliberately introduce to your garden. But if you have this rampant invasive already, its young leaves and shoots are perfectly delicious in salads and as the key ingredient for cold summer soups.

H: 12–24 in (30–60 cm); **S**: indefinite
❀❀❀◊☀☀

Agastache rugosa
This aniseed-scented hardy perennial is easy to grow in most scenarios, although some may find the flavor too strong. A valuable butterfly and bee plant, it is easy to grow from seed and is best treated as an annual in colder zones.

H: 36 in (90 cm); **S**: 12 in (30 cm)
❀◊☀

Ajuga reptans
A traditional medicinal plant with mild properties, bugle is now more commonly grown for the bees and as a colorful ground cover plant. It is easy to propagate and will grow well in shade, but ajuga is not a herb that tolerates drought.

H: 6 in (15 cm); **S**: 24–36 in (60–90 cm) ❀❀❀◐☀

Alcea rosea
Now largely replaced by *Althaea* spp., the hollyhock is a lovely, statuesque perennial best grown as an annual. Let it set seed and it will pop up in the most unlikely spots. It is prone to rust, but a useful plant in the asthma sufferer's garden.

H: 5–8 ft (1.5–2.5 m); **S**: 24 in (60 cm)
❀❀❀◊◐☀

Plant guide (Al–An)

Alchemilla alpina
This handsome dwarf foliage plant is reputedly more effective than *A.mollis* for treating diarrhea and most female ailments, especially menstrual problems. It is easy to grow and compact in form, but it self-seeds and hybridizes readily.

H: 3–5 in (8–12 cm); **S**: 20 in (50 cm)
❄❄❄ ◊ ☼ ☀

Alchemilla mollis
Lady's mantle is easy to grow in most gardens and very useful in mass plantings. Cut back as the flowerheads fade to avoid excessive self-seeding as otherwise *A. mollis* can become a problem. It is beautiful after rain showers.

H: 24 in (60 cm); **S**: 30 in (75 cm)
❄❄❄ ◊ ☼ ☀

Allium sativum
Garlic is one of the most famous of herbs, used worldwide for its varied culinary and medicinal properties. No herb garden should be without it, especially as it is so easy to grow. Plant the bulbs in fall and dig up the following summer.

H: 3 ft (1 m); **S**: 9–12 in (23–30 cm)
❄❄❄ ◊ ☼

Allium schoenoprasum "Forescate"
This clump-forming culinary perennial onion is easily grown and generally trouble-free. The flowers are a colorful addition to salads or as a garnish. Experiment with different cultivars as they vary in size, stature, and strength.

H: 12–24 in (30–60 cm); **S**: 2 in (5 cm)
❄❄❄ ◊ ☼

Allium tuberosum
This culinary and medicinal onion is subtly garlic flavored and more substantial than ordinary chives. It is easy to grow from seed, but when harvesting, leave at least 6 in (15 cm) standing. Divide congested clumps every year.

H: 10–20 in (25–50 cm); **S**: 2 in (5 cm)
❄❄ ◊ ☼

Allium ursinum
Strongly pungent, these woodland natives, commonly known as wild garlic, can be used as a garlic or onion substitute. The flowers are also edible. Useful as a natural insect repellent, but it sets seed readily and can be invasive.

H: 6 in (15 cm); **S**: 6 in (15 cm)
❄❄❄ ◊ ☼ ☀

Aloysia triphylla
Insignificant flowers but this half-hardy shrub has highly fragrant lemon-scented leaves that can be used in teas, jellies, and potpourris. Can be slow to wake up in spring but easy to propagate from softwood cuttings.

H: 10 ft (3 m); **S**: 10 ft (3 m)
❄❄ ◊ ☼ ♈

Althaea officinalis
Marshmallow is a traditional medicinal herb with large velvety leaves and tall spikes of pink or white flowers. Easy to grow from ripe seed in late summer with eratic germination in spring. Also a good butterfly and coastal plant

H: 6 ft (2 m); **S**: 5 ft (1.5 m)
❄❄❄ ◊ ◗ ☼

Amaranthus hypochondriacus
A spectacular culinary and ornamental half-hardy herb with long tassels. Young leaves are good raw in salads and older leaves cooked like cabbage. The seeds are a great wild bird food as well as having myriad culinary attributes.

H: 3–4 ft (0.9–1.2 m); **S**: 12–18 in (30–45 cm) ❄❄ ◗ ☼

Anethum graveolens
Dill is a pungent aromatic culinary and medicinal herb that is easily grown as an annual from seed sown at regular intervals from spring onward. Bolts if stressed but a useful companion plant attracting many beneficial insect predators

H: 24 in (60 cm); **S**: 4 ft (1.2 m)
❄❄❄ ◊ ☼

Angelica archangelica
A massive feature plant best grown as a short-lived perennial that can self-seed freely. Thrives in fertile damp dappled shade and easy to propagate from fresh seed sown in autumn or spring. Young stems can be crystallized or candied.

H: 6 ft (2 m); **S**: 4 ft (1.2 m)
❄❄❄ ◗ ◑ ☀

Anthriscus cerefolium
Chervil is an indispensable culinary herb that really needs to be used fresh to keep its delicate flavor and also has a reputation as aiding the memory. Allegedly a slug repellent, it is easy to grow from seed sown at regular intervals.

H: 20 in (50 cm); **S**: 10 in (24 cm)
❄❄❄ ◊ ☼ ◑

Plant guide (Ar–Bo)

Armeria maritima
Sea thrift is a beautiful low perennial for light, well-drained soils in sun and is ideal for coastal gardens. The pretty pink flowers are borne from early to late summer. The leaves and roots are edible; and the whole dried plant is said to have antibiotic properties.

H: 8 in (20 cm); **S**: 12 in (30 cm)
❋❋❋ ◊ ☼ ♔

Armoracia rusticana
Horseradish is cultivated for its spicy roots, which are collected in the fall; grated, these can be made into horseradish sauce. It is an easy plant to grow from divisions, although owing to its invasive nature, it is best planted on waste ground.

H: 3 ft (1 m); **S**: 18 in (45 cm)
❋❋❋ ◊ ◗ ☼

Arnica montana
This clump-forming yellow flowered perennial has many proven medicinal uses, but it is considered unsafe for taking internally as a medicine. Arnica grows in moist acid soil that is well drained, but is a difficult herb that rarely thrives in lowland plantings.

H: 20 in (50 cm); **S**: 12 in (30 cm)
❋❋❋ ◊ ◗ ☼

Artemisia abrotanum
The aromatic, feathery, gray-green foliage of southernwood makes an excellent moth repellent as well as destroying intestinal worms. It is an easy-to-grow, woody shrub best pruned in late spring to keep it bushy. Tends not to flower in cooler climes.

H: 3 ft (1 m); **S**: 3 ft (1 m)
❋❋❋ ◊ ☼ ♔

Artemisia absinthium
A useful herb for larger containers, but do not feed excessively as the aromatic foliage will turn from silver to green. Wormwood is a natural insect repellent, but it needs some winter protection. This is a herb to avoid if you suffer from hayfever.

H: 36 in (90 cm); **S**: 24 in (60 cm)
❋❋❋ ◊ ☼

Artemisia dracunculus
Tarragon is an essential culinary aromatic herb with a delicate aniseed flavor for which Russian tarragon is no substitute. It is easy to grow and propagate from root cuttings in spring, but needs a warm, dry, sheltered spot to overwinter happily.

H: 4 ft (1.2 m); **S**: 12 in (30 cm)
❋❋❋ ◊ ☼

Artemisia lactiflora
A tall but compact, clump-forming, airy herb with copious plumes of tiny off-white flowers that dry and keep well. A traditional Chinese herb to aid liver function, white mugwort also provides useful border structure if left standing during the winter.

H: 5 ft (1.5 m); **S**: 24 in (60 cm)
❄❄❄ ◊ ☼ ♈

Artemisia ludoviciana
An important aromatic and antiseptic herb in native North American medicine, the light brownish flowers of Western mugwort are bourne in panicles in late summer and the leaves act as a good deodorant in shoes. It thrives in sandy soil.

H: 4 ft (1.2 m); **S**: 24 in (60 cm)
❄❄❄ ◊ ☼

Artemisia pontica
Although this herb has finely cut, silvery-green leaves it is still a drab, dull-looking medicinal herb with similar properties to *A. absinthium*. This species has other useful properties, however, as a flavoring for wines, cordials, and vermouth.

H: 16–32 in (40–80 cm); **S**: indefinite
❄❄❄ ◊ ☼

Asarum canadense
Thriving in a woodland garden, the rhizomes of this evergreen herb are an edible ginger substitute, but its leaves are poisonous. Snake root was widely employed as a medicinal herb by native North American tribes for treating many ailments.

H: 3 in (8 cm); **S**: 12 in (30 cm)
❄❄❄ ◊ ◐ ☼ ☀

Asarum europaeum
With the unusual common name of asarabacca, historically, this herb was useful medicinally, but it is now rarely used. Good as a ground cover plant for the woodland garden, all parts are poisonous when fresh. The leaves do, however, make a vivid green dye.

H: 3 in (8 cm); **S**: 12 in (30 cm)
❄❄❄ ◊ ◐ ☼ ☀ ♈

Borago officinalis
This vividly blue (or white) flowered annual is easy to grow from seed in spring and early summer. The leaves of borage have a delicate, cucumber flavor and the flowers are lovely in drinks and salads. It hates being transplanted, but sets seed freely.

H: 24 in (60 cm); **S**: 18 in (45 cm)
❄❄❄ ◊ ☼ ☀

Plant guide (Ca–Cr)

Calamintha nepeta
Ideal for poor, limey, well-drained soil, this aromatic herb is a must for a bee or butterfly garden. The young leaves are good in a salad and make a fine minty tea. It is tricky to grow from seed but easy from divisions or cuttings.

H: 18 in (45 cm); **S**: 20–30 in (50–75 cm) ❄❄❄ ◊ ◐ ☼ ☀

Calendula officinalis
An easy-to-grow annual with many herbal attributes including antiseptic and fungicidal properties. The young leaves of calendula are edible when fresh and the flower petals make a good dye for rice dishes as well as an interesting tea.

H: 12–28 in (30–70 cm); **S**: 12–18 in (30–45 cm) ❄❄❄ ◊ ☼ ☀

Capsicum annuum
Chili peppers are very variable in shape, color, and strength, so always proceed with some caution when tasting. As a herb, they are used as a food preservative and as a gastrointestinal detoxicant. Very ornamental when in fruit or flower.

H: 5 ft (1.5 m); **S**: 20 in (50 cm) ❄◊ ☼

Carum carvi
Not particularly ornamental, caraway is commercially grown on a large scale for its seed, but the root can be cooked as a vegetable and its leaves eaten in salads. Sow seed in the fall when fresh and grow the herb as a biennial.

H: 24 in (60 cm); **S**: 12 in (30 cm) ❄❄❄ ◊ ☼

Centranthus ruber
Red valerian is an upright perennial that flowers freely for many weeks from late spring to midsummer, attracting bees and butterflies. It prefers chalky or sandy soils and often seeds itself in wall crevices. The edible leaves have culinary uses.

H: 3 ft (1 m); **S**: 3 ft (1 m) ❄❄❄ ◊ ☼

Chamaemelum nobile
The sweet-smelling foliage of lawn chamomile forms a short-lived mat, but the flowers make a classic herbal tea. It is hard work as a lawn, but it looks good in a pot. Trim regularly to prevent it from becoming straggly and having dry, surplus flowers.

H: 12 in (30 cm); **S**: 18 in (45 cm) ❄❄❄ ◊ ☼

Chamaemelum nobile "Treneague"
This non-flowering cultivar of lawn chamomile is easy to grow from offsets, which root very easily—most shoots have some aerial roots. It is easiest to maintain as a small lawn, but it is not drought tolerant, so keep young plants moist in summer.

H: 4 in (10 cm); **S**: 18 in (45 cm)
❄❄❄ ◊ ☀

Chenopodium bonus-henricus
It has insignificant greenish-yellow flowers, but this herb is easy to grow from seed in spring for harvesting the following year. The leaves are good in stuffings and soups, while the young flower spikes are tender and a good asparagus substitute.

H: 32 in (80 cm); **S**: indefinite
❄❄❄ ◊ ◖ ☀ ◑

Cichorium intybus
This herb is a versatile salad plant with the leaves standing well into autumn and early winter. Stunning blue flowers are produced throughout summer. Medicinally it can be used for gout and the roots roasted as a superb coffee substitute.

H: 4 ft (1.2 m); **S**: 24 in (60 cm)
❄❄❄ ◊ ☀

Coriandrum sativum
The whole of this easy-to-grow aromatic plant is edible. Coriander is ideally sown directly in the soil, and if grown in pots, plant out before the taproot has grown out of the rootball—any disturbance will cause the plant to run to seed prematurely.

H: 20 in (50 cm); **S**: 8 in (20 cm)
❄❄❄ ◊ ☀

Crambe maritima
Rich in vitamin C, sea kale is easy to grow from fresh seed sown in the fall and planted out in large pots or in open ground the following year. If the temperature is likely to fall below 34°F (1°C), protect the crown with a thick, dry mulch over winter.

H: 30 in (75 cm); **S**: 24 in (60 cm)
❄❄❄ ◊ ☀ ♈

Crocus sativus
Flowering in winter, crocus styles are commonly used as an exotic food flavoring (saffron) and coloring, but 4,000 stigmas are needed to yield just 1 oz (25 g) of saffron. In climates with cloudier, wetter summers, the bulb will not flower.

H: 2 in (5 cm); **S**: 2 in (5 cm)
❄❄❄ ◊ ☀

Plant guide (Cy–He)

Cynara cardunculus
Medicinal uses for cardoons include liver regeneration and diabetes, but they are primarily grown for their blanched leaves, leaf ribs, and stalks. They can be grown from seed, but for reliable cropping, divisions from selected plants is preferable.

H: 5 ft (1.5 m); **S**: 4 ft (1.2 m)
❄❄❄ ◊ ☼ ♉

Echinacea purpurea
Echinacea is easy to grow from seed in spring and to propagate from division in late fall. The flowers and dried roots from older plants are extensively used in modern herbal medicine—in the past, they were also used as a snakebite antidote.

H: 5 ft (1.5 m); **S**: 18 in (45 cm)
❄❄❄ ◊ ☼

Ferula communis
This enormous, highly effective aromatic herb is best grown at the back of a border as a feature plant. It is preferable to remove flowerheads to prevent seed setting as it often dies after flowering. Once established, plants dislike disturbance.

H: 6–10 ft (2–3 m); **S**: 24 in (60 cm)
❄❄ ◊ ☼

Filipendula ulmaria
All parts of meadowseet are traditionally used for an acidic stomach, and it is easily grown in the garden as well as the wild flower meadow. The almond-scented flowers add flavor to wines and non-alcoholic herbal punches.

H: 24–36 in (60–90 cm); **S**: 24 in (60 cm) ❄❄❄ ◊ ◗ ☼ ☼

Filipendula vulgaris
With larger flowers than *F. ulmaria*, this is a very good bee plant and is said to be resistant to browsing by deer. Thriving on chalk soils, it dislikes dry acid sites. Dropwort is easy to propagate by dividing congested clumps in late fall.

H: 24 in (60 cm); **S**: 18 in (45 cm)
❄❄❄ ◊ ◗ ☼ ☼

Foeniculum vulgare
Fennel is a staple herb for both the ornamental and culinary garden. For a delicate, aniseed flavor, use green fennel foliage with fatty meat dishes, fish, and in salads. It will tolerate poor conditions, but will really show off if treated well.

H: 6 ft (1.8 m); **S**: 18 in (45 cm)
❄❄❄ ◊ ◗ ☼

Foeniculum vulgare **var.** *dulce*

While the seeds and feathery leaves can be used as a herb, this species of fennel is grown as a single-stemmed annual for its bulbous base, which can be roasted whole or grated into salads. A tea made from the seeds will help digestion.

H: 6 ft (1.8 m); **S**: 18 in (45 cm)
❄❄❄ ◊ ◊ ☼

Foeniculum vulgare "*Purpureum*"

The striking bronze feathery leaves of this cultivar can be used as for *Foeniculum vulgare*. Take care not to grow this herb near dill or any other species of fennel as cross pollination of these prolific seed producers will most likely occur.

H: 6 ft (1.8 m); **S**: 18 in (45 cm)
❄❄❄ ◊ ◊ ☼

Galium odoratum

Sweet woodruff is a very useful aromatic herb for underplanting dry, shady areas. The leaves and flowers give up their best aromas when dried and added to potpourris. Fresh flowers are good in salads and the leaves make a tea to aid indigestion.

H: 18 in (45 cm); **S**: indefinite
❄❄❄ ◊ ☼ ☼

Hamamelis virginiana

The autumnal flowers of Virginian witch hazel have a lovely sweet aroma, but it is the bark that is used to produce medicinal remedies for gastric problems and internal bleeding as well as witch hazel drops for eye and skin treatments.

H: 12 ft (4 m); **S**: 12 ft (4 m)
❄❄❄ ◊ ◊ ☼ ☼

Hedeoma pulegioides **syn.** *Mentha pulegioides*

A strongly pungent and aromatic annual, use this herb in moderation for flavoring and as a mint tea. It is commercially used to produce insect repellent and the leaves may repel insects if rubbed on the skin.

H: 12 in (30 cm); **S**: 6 in (15 cm)
❄❄❄ ◊ ☼

Helichrysum italicum

On warm days, this striking silver-foliaged plant exudes a strong curry scent, but is little use as flavoring except perhaps as a garnish on steamed rice. It is easy to propagate from semi-ripe cuttings in the fall and makes a good edging plant.

H: 24 in (60 cm); **S**: 3 ft (1 m)
❄❄ ◊ ☼ ♈

Plant guide (He–La)

Hesperis matronalis
Sweet rocket is an attractive herb that produces a lovely clovelike sweet scent in early evening. The leaves are a little bitter but can be used in salads in moderation. Easy to grow from seed and a good drought-resistant, bee, butterfly, and moth plant.

H: 36 in (90 cm); **S**: 18 in (45 cm)
❆❆❆ ◊ ◖ ☼ ☀

Humulus lupulus
The easy-to-grow hop is of great economic importance globally in the brewing industry and is a superb vigorous climber in the garden. Feed it well and ensure the plant is kept under control as spreading suckers can become a problem.

H: 20 ft (6 m)
❆❆❆ ◊ ◖ ☼ ☀

Hypericum perforatum
Mainly grown as an ornamental shrub, this herb was historically a bit of a "cure-all," but is now used to treat neuralgia and sunburn. Giving off a nasty aroma when handled, it is poisonous to livestock so should not be grown on boundaries.

H: 24–42 in (60–110 cm); **S**: 24 in (60 cm) ❆❆❆ ◊ ◖ ☼ ☀

Hyssopus officinalis
Useful as an alternative low hedging plant if kept well trimmed, the blue spikes of hyssop are very attractive to bees and butterflies. Deadhead regularly to promote flowering. Use sparingly in fatty stews and soups or add the flowers to salads.

H: 24 in (60 cm); **S**: 3 ft (1 m)
❆❆❆ ◊ ☼

Hyssopus officinalis f. albus
This pure white flowered cultivar is as aromatic and useful as the blue but, to ensure white progeny, must be propagated by softwood cuttings in summer. Growing from seed is easy in spring, but may yield blue, white, or pink flowered plants.

H: 24 in (60 cm); **S**: 3 ft (1 m)
❆❆❆ ◊ ☼

Hyssopus officinalis "Roseus"
Contrasts well with gray leaved plants and, as with the blue and white forms, can be renovated if it becomes straggly or ungainly by cutting back hard in spring. Propagate by softwood cuttings or, if color is unimportant, by seed in spring.

H: 24 in (60 cm); **S**: 3 ft (1 m)
❆❆❆ ◊ ☼

Inula helenium
Elecampane is a statuesque giant among large perennial herbs that dies back below ground in winter. It is little used as a herb today, but was important to the Romans. The candied roots are edible and smell of ripe bananas when harvested.

H: 3–6 ft (0.9–2 m); **S**: 36 in (90 cm)
✻✻✻ ◊ ◖ ☼

Jasminum humile
A useful slightly scented scrambler for dappled shade, the leaves and bark can be used for a tea. The roots have been used as a cure for intestinal worms. Almost evergreen, some protection over winter may be needed in colder climates.

H: 00 in (00 cm); **S**: 00 in (00 cm)
✻✻ ◊ ☼

Jasminum officinale
The flowers of this vigorous climber are deliciously scented and used in perfumery as well as eaten or dried for use as a tea substitute. Some protection may be needed in colder areas until established. Do not use the poisonous berries.

H: 40 ft (12 m)
✻✻ ◊ ☼ ◑☼ ♈

Jasminum sambac
In cool areas, grow this tender climber under cover or in a conservatory. It is tolerant of light shade and grows well in containers if kept barely moist. The scented flowers are used in teas, for flavoring deserts, and in perfumery.

H: 6–10 ft (2–3 m)
✻◊ ☼ ◑☼ ♈

Juniperus communis
This slow-growing, large conifer is extensively used for both medicinal and culinary purposes, including the production of gin. However, in excess, it can cause renal damage and should not be used in any quantity by pregnant women.

H: 1½–20 ft (0.5–6 m); **S**: 3–20 ft (1–6 m) ✻✻✻ ◊ ☼ ☼

Laurus nobilis
The dried leaves are widely used in cooking, but fresh leaves taste better. Easy to grow in containers, but will need regular repotting and keeping barely moist over winter. The leaves are a deterrent to weevils, but bay is prone to attack by scale insects.

H: 40 ft (12 m); **S**: 30 ft (10 m)
✻✻ ◊ ◖ ☼ ◑☼ ♈

Plant guide (*Lavandula*)

Lavandula angustifolia "Hidcote"
This classic lavender is grown for its dark purple flower spikes that appear from midsummer. It makes a wonderful hedge. The aromatic leaves have a wide range of medicinal uses, although it is the essential oil that is most commonly used.

H: 24 in (60 cm); **S**: 24 in (60 cm)
❄❄❄ ◊ ◖ ☼ ♈

Lavandula angustifolia "Munstead"
Another popular lavender with purple-blue flower spikes. Because lavenders are evergreen, their strongly aromatic foliage can be appreciated year-round. Its long-lasting scent has a soothing and relaxing effect.

H: 24 in (60 cm); **S**: 24 in (60 cm)
❄❄❄ ◊ ◊ ☼

Lavandula angustifolia "Royal Purple"
A fine cultivar of lavender, chosen for its long purple flowerheads from midsummer. Like other lavenders, the fresh or dried flowers can be used as a flavoring for tea, jams, ice creams, vinegars, or oils. The leaves are also used as a cooking or salad ingredient.

H: 30 in (75 cm); **S**: 24 in (60 cm)
❄❄❄ ◊ ◖ ☼

Lavandula canariensis
This lavender from the Canary Islands needs protection in winter if it is to live from one year to the next. But the effort this takes is rewarded with stunningly vivid blue flowers in summer set against the the form's bright green leaves.

H: 24 in (60 cm); **S**: 24 in (60 cm)
❄◊ ☼

Lavandula x *ginginsii* "Goodwin Creek Gray"
Very long, purple flowers are borne throughout much of summer above the velvety foliage of this lavender. Unlike others, the sweet-scented, silvery leaves are fairly wide and toothed. The flowers are not edible.

H: 36 in (90 cm); **S**: 36 in (90 cm)
❄◊ ☼

Lavandula x *intermedia* "Impress Purple"
This hybrid lavender shares the same qualities as *L. angustifolia*, although it is a taller, more bushy plant with sprawling stems. When in full flower, there is a beautiful cloud of purple rising above the silvery green foliage.

H: 3 ft (1 m); **S**: 5 ft (1.5 m)
❄❄❄ ◊ ◖ ☼

Lavandula lanata
Woolly lavender is known for its downy, silvery-gray foliage with the characteristic lavender scent and herbal properties. To grow well, it needs to be protected from winter wet to prevent the roots from rotting. The flowers appear in midsummer.

H: 20 in (50 cm); **S**: 24 in (60 cm)
❄❄ ◊ ◑ ☼ ♈

Lavandula pendunculata subsp. pendunculata
Spanish lavender is a very desirable plant for the ornamental herb garden. In midsummer, its flowerheads are topped by long, pale purple petals that look like they are floating above the pale green foliage.

H: 30 in (75 cm); **S**: 24 in (60 cm)
❄❄ ◊ ☼ ♈

Lavandula pinnata
This frost-tender lavender cannot survive frosty winters, yet it makes a good windowsill herb, either for the greenhouse or kitchen. The finely toothed leaves are quite distinctive and the vivid blue flowers in summer are exquisite.

H: 24 in (60 cm); **S**: 24 in (60 cm)
❄◊ ☼

Lavandula stoechas
French lavender is grown for its silvery aromatic leaves, used for essential oils, as incense, for potpourri, and sometimes as an insect repellent. The flowers steal the show with their distinctive "ears" of purple sprouting from each flowerhead.

H: 24 in (60 cm); **S**: 24 in (60 cm)
❄❄ ◊ ☼ ♈

Lavandula stoechas "With Love"
Several cultivars of French lavender exist, chosen purely for ornamental reasons. "With Love" has long, pale purple "ears." "Kew Red" has reddish purple flowers, although it dislikes wet soil in winter and will die in all but the most free-draining of soils.

H: 24 in (60 cm); **S**: 24 in (60 cm)
❄❄ ◊ ☼

Lavandula viridis
Green or lemon lavender is highly aromatic with lush green leaves. The white flowers appear in late spring followed by successive flushes throughout the summer. It is easy to propagate from softwood cuttings in summer or seed sown in spring.

H: 24 in (60 cm); **S**: 24 in (60 cm)
❄❄ ◊ ☼

Plant guide (Le–Me)

Levisticum officinale
Lovage is a substantial perennial that is very easy to grow from seed in spring, but needs plenty of space. Makes lovely soup on its own and the seeds and its young celery-scented leaves can be added to salads. Cut back in midsummer to rejuvenate.

H: 6 ft (2 m); **S**: 3 ft (1 m)
❄❄❄ ◌ ◖ ☼

Ligusticum scoticum
Scots or sea lovage is useful in maritime areas and is more compact and not as strongly scented as *Levisticum officinale*. It can be grown in a large container, but will not tolerate shade. Sow seed when fresh in the fall.

H: 15–24 in (38–60 cm); **S**: 16 in (40 cm) ❄❄❄ ◌ ☼

Lonicera pericylmenum
This sweetly scented, vigorous climber is very useful in the partially shaded garden and its flowers can be used in salads and potpourris. The berries are toxic and should not be eaten. Old plants can be renovated by cutting back hard in early spring.

H: 22 ft (7 m)
❄❄❄ ◌ ◖ ☼ ◐

Melilotus officinalis
A saline-tolerant biennial herb best grown in a wildflower meadow as it is very attractive to bees. Fresh leaves are a good flavoring for stews and salads, but dried leaves can be toxic. It dies after flowering, so best grown as an annual from seed in spring.

H: 5 ft (1.5 m); **S**: 12 in (30 cm)
❄◌ ☼

Melissa officinalis "All Gold"
The lemon-scented leaves of lemon balm are widely used as food flavorings as well as in many cordials and liqueurs. It makes a lovely tea and the whole plant can act as an insect repellent. Self-seeds prolifically, so cut back as the tiny flowers fade.

H: 2–4 ft (60–120 cm); **S**: 12–18 in (30–45 cm) ❄❄❄ ◌ ☼

Melissa officinalis "Aurea"
This variegated, beautifully aromatic cultivar is a more compact clump-former then *M. officinalis* and does not set seed quite so vigorously, but it is just as useful in the kitchen. Reversion to plain green can occur over time.

H: 2–4 ft (60–120 cm); **S**: 12–18 in (30–45 cm) ❄❄❄ ◌ ☼

Mentha x piperita f. citrata

Lemon mint is too aromatic for many people, but makes lovely herbal teas and iced drinks. It is widely used commercially in the perfumery and pharmaceutical industries and is easy to grow, although it needs containerizing as can be invasive.

H: 20 in (50 cm); **S**: 3 ft (1 m)
❄❄❄ ◊ ◕ ☼

Mentha x piperita "Logee's"

Grown in a pot, this is a lovely, more compact green and white variegated cultivar. The leaves are strongly spearmint flavored and can be used in cooking as well as fresh or dried to make a flavorsome tea that aids the digestion.

H: 20 in (50 cm); **S**: 3 ft (1 m)
❄❄❄ ◊ ◕ ☼

Mentha pulegium

Historically an important medicinal herb, pennyroyal can be used as a digestive tonic, but must be avoided by pregnant women. This herb is easy to grow from seed and its spearmint-like flavor is useful in potpourris. It is also a useful ground cover plant.

H: 4–16 in (10–40 cm); **S**: 20 in (50 cm) ❄❄❄ ◊ ◕ ☼

Mentha requienii

Corsican mint is robust, vigorous, ground hugging, and tiny leaved, ideal for filling cracks in pavement. It releases a lovely scent when crushed and will tolerate being walked on. Best propagated by division and over wintered in a sheltered spot.

H: ½ in (1 cm); **S**: indefinite
❄❄❄ ◊ ◕ ☼ ☼

Mentha spicata

Spearmint has a very refreshing, clean flavor. Often used in making mint sauce, jellies, and tea, it is a good bee plant, but repellent to other insects, rats, and mice. It should ideally be planted in a container as it spreads rapidly in open ground.

H: 3 ft (1 m); **S**: indefinite
❄❄❄ ◊ ◕ ☼

Mentha x villosa var. alopecuroides Bowles's mint

A flavorsome, mauve flowered, large mint that is best grown in a restricted space or container. Easily propagated from root cuttings or congested clumps, it can be lifted and divided when in active growth.

H: 12–36 in (30–90 cm); **S**: indefinite
❄❄❄ ◊ ◕ ☼

Plant guide (Mo–Oc)

Monarda didyma
Native to North America, the edible flowers of bee balm look stunning in a salad and the fresh or dried leaves make the herbal classic oswego tea. Very attractive to butterflies, it is easy to grow but short lived and can be propagated by division in spring.

H: 36 in (90 cm); **S**: 18 in (45 cm)
❄❄❄ ◌◌ ☼ ☼

Monarda fistulosa
Historically, wild bee balm is widely used for digestive and bronchial disorders. The fresh leaves have a sweet, oreganolike flavor and can be used in meat dishes or as a herbal tea. Happy in heavy soils, it will not tolerate dryness or drought.

H: 4 ft (1.2 m); **S**: 18 in (45 cm)
❄❄❄ ◌◌ ☼ ☼

Murraya koenigii
Grow in a large container as a conservatory or houseplant, the aromatic leaves are used to make curry powder and the peppery red fruits can be used as a seasoning. It is slow growing and can be fickle, but is worth the effort.

H: 10 ft (3 m); **S**: 10 ft (3 m)
❄◌ ☼

Myrrhis odorata
Sweet Cicely is easy to grow from fresh seed or divisions and the delicate aniseed-flavored leaves are good in salads and as a sweetener in acidic stewed fruits. The seeds are a good breath freshener if chewed; for the best flavor, gather when green.

H: 6 ft (2 m); **S**: 5 ft (1.5 m)
❄❄❄ ◌ ☼

Myrtus communis
A useful evergreen shrub, myrtle's aromatic leaves can be used fresh or dried in stews and game dishes as well as potpourris. It is quite tender but will survive some frosts if over wintered in a sheltered spot and protected from excessive wet.

H: 10 ft (3 m); **S**: 10 ft (3 m)
❄❄ ◌◌ ☼ ⚆

Nepeta cataria
Cats either love this aromatic herb or are totally indifferent, hence its common name of cat nip. The leaves act as an insect repellent in the vegetable garden while the tall flower spikes are a useful addition to the flower border.

H: 12 in (30 cm); **S**: 12 in (30 cm)
❄❄❄ ◌ ☼ ☼

Ocimum basilicum **"Cinnamon"**
Like all basils, this cultivar is easy to grow but best if treated like a tender annual and sown in pots in a warm, well-ventilated spot. Cinnamon-scented, purple-veined leaves can be added to spicy stir fries or salad dressings. Attractive flowerheads.

H: 12–24 in (30–60 cm); **S**: 12 in (30 cm) ❋◊ ☼

Ocimum basilicum **"Dark Opal"**
The highly aromatic dark leaves of "Dark Red Opal" have many culinary uses, but are best used where the color will contrast with other ingredients in salads, pasta, and rice dishes. It grows well in a deep pot with sharply draining compost.

H: 12–24 in (30–60 cm); **S**: 12 in (30 cm) ❋◊ ☼

Ocimum basilicum **"Lettuce Leaved"**
Very aromatic and sweet, the large leaves are useful for wrapping around feta cheese or cherry tomatoes. Needs more space than the smaller-leaved cultivars. Keep pinching out tips or trimming back to ensure a continual supply of young leaves.

H: 12–24 in (30–60 cm); **S**: 12 in (30 cm) ❋◊ ☼

Ocimum basilicum **var.** *purpurascens* **"Red Rubin"**
A spectacular, deep purple, strongly-scented leaf. As with all basils, this herb will not tolerate excess wetness, so water in the early morning and do not allow to stand in water over night. It also needs a sheltered spot.

H: 12–24 in (30–60 cm); **S**: 12 in (30 cm) ❋◊ ☼

Ocimum basilicum **x** *citriodorum* **"Siam Queen"**
The mulberry-colored flower bracts are very attractive, but need to be pinched out to ensure a supply of the slightly aniseed-flavored fresh leaves. It is superb as a container plant on the patio.

H: 12–24 in (30–60 cm); **S**: 12 in (30 cm) ❋◊ ☼

Ocimum basilicum **"Sweet Thai"**
The sweetly-scented leaves with a hint of liquorice are used in Thai curries—often added by the handful. It is best grown as an annual from seed sown in spring and early summer. "Sweet Thai" will not tolerate drought or sitting in cold water.

H: 12–24 in (30–60 cm); **S**: 12 in (30 cm) ❋◊ ☼

Plant guide (Or–Pr)

Origanum dictamnus

A drought-tolerant, prostrate or mound-forming shrubby herb that will not stand excessive wet. Use the aromatic woolly leaves of hop marjoram as a dried seasoning mixed with parsley, thyme, and garlic. The flowering tips make a calming tea.

H: 6 in (15 cm); **S**: 8 in (20 cm)
❄❄ ◊ ☼

Origanum laevigatum "Herrenhausen"

The dark green leaves and purple stems and flowers of this robust, fully hardy oregano (or marjoram) make a strikingly good contrast in the herb garden and the leaves substitute very well for the less ornamental or fickle forms of *Origanum*.

H: 18 in (45 cm); **S**: 18 in (45 cm)
❄❄❄ ◊ ☼ ♈

Origanum "Kent Beauty"

A unpredictable herb that rewards the effort with beautifully ruffled flower bracts above aromatic leaves on trailing stems. Not tolerant of winter wet, but it grows well in screelike conditions and is attractive to bees and butterflies.

H: 4 in (10 cm); **S**: 8 in (20 cm)
❄❄❄ ◊ ☼

Origanum vulgare "Acorn Bank"

Wild marjoram is an easily grown, spreading kitchen herb that suits most soils in sun, although golden-leaved varieties tolerate partial shade. The uses are mostly culinary, being an important flavoring in many Mediterranean dishes.

H: 18 in (45 cm); **S**: indefinite
❄❄❄ ◊ ☼ ☀

Origanum vulgare "Aureum"

This golden-leaved variety of wild marjoram is in particular need of partial shade if it is to grow well. It can be used in the kitchen as for all other varieties and its medicinal uses are as an antiseptic and as an essential oil in aromatherapy.

H: 18 in (45 cm); **S**: indefinite
❄❄❄ ◊ ☀ ♈

Origanum vulgare "Polyphant"

A darker-leaved variety of wild marjoram, each one with a narrow, cream-colored edge. An unusual variety for the kitchen herb border. Like other varieties of marjoram, the flowers are pink and small, appearing from midsummer.

H: 18 in (45 cm); **S**: indefinite
❄❄❄ ◊ ☼

Petroselinum crispum
An essential culinary herb for garnishing and flavoring, curly-leaved parsley is easy to grow from seed. Deadhead and trim regularly to ensure a succession of succulent leaves, which are a useful relief to garlic breathe.

H: 32 in (80 cm); **S**: 24 in (60 cm)
❄❄❄ ◌ ◑ ☼ ☼

Petroselinum crispum "Italian"
Flat-leaved parsley resents transplanting or root disturbance, so it is best grown in modules or directly into the ground. Good in deep containers, parsley is a hungry herb and needs regular feeding. Sow a fresh batch annually.

H: 32 in (80 cm); **S**: 24 in (60 cm)
❄❄❄ ◌ ◑ ☼ ☼

Pimpinella anisum
Traditionally used as an aphrodisiac, this aromatic annual is now used as the anise flavoring in various liquors. *Pimpinella anisum* is not particularly ornamental, but it is easy to grow and useful in companion planting to reduce aphid and insect problems.

H: 4 ft (1.2 m); **S**: 24 in (60 cm)
❄❄❄ ◌ ◑ ☼ ☼

Plectranthus amboinicus
This highly aromatic, camphorous- or oregano-scented tender herb is easy to grow as a houseplant with a minimum temperature of 50°F (10°C). The leaves are good with chicken and rice dishes and also have some antiseptic properties.

H: 12 in (30 cm); **S**: 3 ft (1 m)
❄◌ ☼

Portulaca oleracea
The leaves of pigweed are very succulent and a rich source of omega-3 fatty acids. Sow seed in modules or directly in the ground in spring. For salads, regularly harvest fresh young leaves and seedheads, cutting from the tips not the sides.

H: 4–8 in (10–20 cm); **S**: 6 in (15 cm)
❄❄ ◌ ☼

Primula veris
A once common wildflower in meadows, primroses are now protected in many countries. Young leaves and flowers are good in salads and a fine wine, and herbal tea can be brewed from the flowers. Divide in the fall or propagate from seed.

H: 10 in (25 cm); **S**: 10 in (25 cm)
❄❄❄ ◌ ◑ ☼ ☼ ♚

Plant guide (Rh–Sa)

Rheum palmatum
While the leaves of all rhubarbs are poisonous, the rhizomes of Chinese rhubarb have been used extensively in herbal medicine. The stems are not edible, but this statuesque plant is a very useful feature with its long leaves and tall flower stems.

H: 8 ft (2.5 m); **S**: 6 ft (1.8 m)
❄❄❄ ◗ ☼ ☀

Ribes nigrum "Ben Connan"
All parts of this widely grown culinary shrub are highly aromatic and its fruits are high in vitamin C and used in cordials and liquors. Dried blackcurrant leaves make a good tea and an infusion from dried berries is a good mouthwash or gargle.

H: 3 ft (1 m); **S**: 3 ft (1 m)
❄❄❄ ◌ ☼ ♛

Rosa canina
Not very valuable as an ornamental rose, the fresh hips of dog rose make good wines, jams, and syrups as well as being quite tasty raw, but remove the irritant seed hairs just beneath the fruit flesh. Rosehip tea is made from macerated hips.

H: 10 ft (3 m)
❄❄❄ ◌ ☼

Rosmarinus officinalis
This evergreen aromatic shrub is an essential component of any herb garden. Easy to grow in most moist but well-drained soils, it will thrive in a container that is deeper than it is broad. However, once planted it doesn't like being moved.

H: 5 ft (1.5 m); **S**: 5 ft (1.5 m)
❄❄ ◌ ☼

Rosmarinus officinalis "Miss Jessopp's Upright"
An erect variety, useful for informal hedges, whose fleshier, short, dark leaves are superb with lamb, soups, and stews. Use fresh young sprigs for the best flavor, but it can be dried for storage.

H: 6 ft (2 m); **S**: 6 ft (2 m)
❄❄ ◌ ☼ ♛

Rosmarinus officinalis "Roseus"
Seed collected in late summer is unlikely to come true, so propagate from cuttings in summer. The pink flowers are aromatic and can be used in salads and garnishes. Only prune in early summer, preferably immediately after flowering in the spring.

H: 5 ft (1.5 m); **S**: 5 ft (1.5 m)
❄❄ ◌ ☼

Rosmarinus **Prostratus Group**
A very useful sprawling aromatic herb that is good trailing over walls or out of containers and hanging baskets. As with all rosemary, it is attractive to bees and butterflies. Be careful not to disrupt the shape and form when harvesting or pruning in spring.

H: 6 in (15 cm); **S**: 5 ft (1.5 m)
❋❋ ◊ ☼ ♔

Rumex acetosa
Dock is very easy to grow from seed sown in spring. The acidic, young, lemony-flavored leaves are good used sparingly in salads or, when older and tougher, used to make soups and sauces. For a steady supply, harvest or cut back regularly.

H: 24 in (60 cm); **S**: 12 in (30 cm)
❋❋❋ ◊ ☼

Rumex scutatus
French sorrel is a good culinary herb, grown for its strongly flavored leaves that have an acidic lemon flavor. Use sparingly and sufferers of rheumatism, gout, or arthritis should avoid this plant. It is sprawling and makes good ground cover.

H: 36 in (90 cm); **S**: 12 in (30 cm)
❋❋❋ ◊ ◊ ☼

Ruscus aculeatus
The young shoots of this evergreen are mildly laxative and can be eaten as an asparagus substitute. It is best planted as an informal boundary hedge, as when mature, its spine-tipped leaves tend to be disliked by rabbits and other invaders.

H: 30 in (75 cm); **S**: 3 ft (1 m)
❋❋❋ ◊ ◊ ☼ ☼ ☀

Ruta graveolens "Variegata"
Common rue is a very attractive evergreen plant that can be used as a culinary herb but is incredibly bitter. The foliage can cause severe allergic reactions if handled, so wear gloves and site the plant well out of reach of children.

H: 3 ft (1 m); **S**: 30 in (75 cm)
❋❋❋ ◊ ☼ ☀

Salix alba
A large tree whose leaves and bark have been extensively used medicinally as the precursor to aspirin. In smaller gardens, pollard willow to show its colorful young stems and it is very useful in moist or wet soil near watercourses or ponds.

H: 80 ft (25 m); **S**: 30 ft (10 m)
❋❋❋ ◊ ◊ ☼

Plant guide (Sal–San)

Salvia argentea
Silver sage is a foliage herb valued for its rosettes of large, silvery, hairy leaves that look impressive planted along the front of a herb border. It dies in its second year after flowering; Flowers are usually removed, but if left, the plant may self-seed.

H: 18 in (45 cm); **S**: 18 in (45 cm)
❆❆ ◊ ☼ ♟

Salvia clevelandii
Jim sage has pleasantly flavored and aromatic leaves that can be used as a substitute for common sage in cooking. It is an evergreen shrub with pinkish-blue whorls of flower clusters held well above the foliage in summer. It is attractive to bees.

H: 3 ft (1 m); **S**: 24 in (60 cm)
❆❆ ◊ ☼

Salvia discolor
Andean sage is a native of Peru and its scandent habit enables its silver-backed blackcurrant-scented green leaves to be appreciated. Thin sticky stems support the almost black flowers. Some staking is needed and over winter in a cool greenhouse.

H: 3 ft (1 m); **S**: 3 ft (1 m)
❆◊ ☼ ☼ ♟

Salvia elegans "Scarlet Pineapple"
Pineapple sage is popular for its green, pineapple-scented leaves that can be used as a flavoring to savory dishes, salads, or drinks. In late summer, this variety carries bright red, trumpet-shaped flowers above the foliage.

H: 36 in (90 cm); **S**: 36 in (90 cm)
❆❆ ◊ ◖ ☼

Salvia officinalis
Common sage is a lovely evergreen shrubby herb, grown for its soft green, aromatic foliage, which has long been used as a medicine and in the kitchen. It is said to be an aid to digestion and can be made into a herb tea or added to savory dishes.

H: 30 in (75 cm); **S**: 30 in (75 cm)
❆❆ ◊ ☼

Salvia officinalis "Icterina"
This variegated form of common sage has pale green and yellow leaves and has the same uses in the herb garden as the species. Medicinally, sage is credited as making a good antiseptic mouthwash, and in small doses can be taken internally to treat various ills.

H: 30 in (75 cm); **S**: 3 ft (1 m)
❆❆ ◊ ☼ ♟

Salvia officinalis **"Purpurascens"**
Many herbalists believe the purple-leaved form of common sage to be the most potent form. It has been used to treat anxiety and depression, insect bites, and skin and mouth infections. Purple-blue flowers may appear in summer.

H: 30 in (75 cm); **S**: 3 ft (1 m)
❄❄ ◊ ☼ ♈

Salvia officinalis **"Tricolor"**
A popular sage with variegated leaves that are tinged red when young. These are always eye-catching in the ornamental herb garden as well as in the kitchen when used fresh. Sages are drought tolerant, but they benefit from extra water during dry periods.

H: 30 in (75 cm); **S**: 3 ft (1 m)
❄❄ ◊ ☼

Salvia sclarea
Clary sage is biennial, growing grayish, textured, and aromatic leaves in the first summer and then white and purple-blue flowers late in the second summer before dying. These are attractive to bees. The leaves are used in the kitchen and medicinally.

H: 24 in (60 cm); **S**: 12 in (30 cm)
❄❄❄ ◊ ☼

Sanguisorba minor
Easy to grow from seed in late spring, the leaves of small burnet have a delicate cucumber flavor and can be added to salads or dried to make a herbal tea. Trim to reduce flowering and to promote a continuous supply of fresh young leaves.

H: 4 ft (1.2 m); **S**: 24 in (60 cm)
❄❄❄ ◊ ◖ ☼ ☼

Santolina chamaecyparissus **"Lemon Queen"**
Cotton lavender is an aromatic gray-leaved shrub that makes a good alternative to box as a low hedging. It is vital to cut back after flowering. Propagation is easy by semi-ripe cuttings in late summer.

H: 24 in (60 cm); **S**: 24 in (60 cm)
❄❄ ◊ ☼

Santolina chamaecyparissus **"Pretty Carol"**
Regular trimming of this gray-green foliaged cultivar keeps it in shape, but do not trim in the fall as winter cold and wet could cause severe damage. The dried leaves are a moth repellent and can be added to potpourris.

H: 16 in (40 cm); **S**: 16 in (40 cm)
❄❄ ◊ ☼

Plant guide (Sap–Ta)

Saponaria officinalis
Soapwort is an attractive herb that was widely used medicinally, but should only be administered under a qualified herbalist's orders. The crushed roots and leaves can be used as a shampoo for textiles. Best grown in a container as can be invasive.

H: 24 in (60 cm); **S**: 20 in (50 cm)
✽✽✽ ◊ ☼

Satureja hortensis
Grow each summer from seed sown in spring, summer savory germinates readily growing into a bushy plant whose leaves are a useful seasoning for meat dishes. Medicinally it can be used sparingly for a range of gastrointestinal disorders.

H: 10 in (25 cm); **S**: 12 in (30 cm)
✽✽ ◊ ☼

Satureja montana
Winter savory is a hardy perennial that is a useful edging plant. It bushier than *S. hortensis* and has a stronger, more pungent flavor, so should be used in moderation. Cut back established plants in spring to promote vigorous, fresh growth.

H: 16 in (40 cm); **S**: 8 in (20 cm)
✽✽✽ ◊ ☼

Satureja spicigera
This low-growing, late flowering prostrate shrublet combines well with thymes and basils in the herb garden and is a good bee and butterfly plant. When rubbed on the skin, the fresh leaves provide relief from irritant insect stings.

H: 6 in (15 cm); **S**: 12 in (30 cm)
✽✽✽ ◊ ☼

Sempervivum tectorum
Drought resistant and fully hardy, this fleshy-leaved herb is rarely used nowadays for internal complaints, but if macerated, the leaves provide strong relief from burns, stings, and itches. Easy to grow and propagate from seeds or offset divisions.

H: 6 in (15 cm); **S**: 20 in (50 cm)
✽✽✽ ◊ ☼ ♆

Stachys officinalis
This hairy, rhizomatic perennial naturalizes well in wildflower meadows and is easy to grow from seed sown in fall or spring. It is little used medicinally nowadays, but the flowers and leaves can be used to make an invigorating herbal tea.

H: 24 in (60 cm); **S**: 12 in (30 cm)
✽✽✽ ◊ ☼

Symphytum "Goldsmith"
A more compact, sprawling, variegated species of *Symphytum* that can be invasive if not kept under control. The hairy leaves of comfrey are an irritant, so cover the skin before handling the foliage. It is useful in the wild, woodland garden.

H: 12 in (30 cm); **S**: 12 in (30 cm)
❄❄❄ ◊ ◑ ☼ ☀

Symphytum officinale
Common comfrey is a large, easy-to-grow perennial that is an essential addition to any herb garden. Useful as a compost activator and as a liquid feed. Historically an important medicinal herb, but do not use internally today.

H: 5 ft (1.5 m); **S**: 6 ft (2 m)
❄❄❄ ◊ ◑ ☼ ☀

Symphytum x uplandicum
A very tall comfrey species only suitable as an ornamental in the larger garden, but can be grown as a plant food in the vegetable patch. Steep the leaves in water for 28 days or until decayed and dilute well before applying to food crops.

H: 6 ft (2 m); **S**: 4 ft (1.2 m)
❄❄❄ ◊ ◑ ☼ ☀

Tagetes "Lemon Gem"
The whole plant is aromatic with a lemon scent, especially when the leaves are crushed. An easy-to-grow, spring-sown annual, marigold has some insect-repellent properties and is allegedly effective against soil-borne nematodes.

H: 9 in (23 cm); **S**: 16 in (40 cm)
❄◊ ☼

Tagetes lucida
Known as Spanish tarragon, this is a tender perennial that is unlikely to flower in colder climates. Grow from seed in a container and over winter in a sheltered site. The leaves are aniseed flavored and a stronger tasting alternative to tarragon.

H: 36 in (90 cm); **S**: 12 in (30 cm)
❄◊ ☼

Tagetes patula
A tall annual whose leaves have a refreshing pungent smell. Can be used in companion planting as it is reputed to control white fly, nematodes, ground elder, bindweed, and couch grass. If planting with tomatoes, select a compact cultivar.

H: 6–12 in (15–30 cm); **S**: 16 in (40 cm) ❄◊ ☼

Plant guide (Ta–Th)

Tanacetum balsamita
Historically used in the brewing industry to clarify ales, the aromatic, slightly mint-scented leaves are a moth repellent and useful addition to potpourris. Seed is not reliably viable, so best propagated by division in spring or fall.

H: 36 in (90 cm); **S**: 18 in (45 cm)
✲✲✲ ◌ ☼

Tanacetum parthenium
This compact, short-lived aromatic perennial can become a problem if not deadheaded to prevent self-seeding. Feverfew tastes disgusting, but can be used externally to relieve insect stings. Very easy to propagate by stem cuttings or division.

H: 18–24 in (45–60 cm); **S**: 12 in (30 cm) ✲✲✲ ◌ ☼

Tanacetum vulgare
Common tansy is a tall perennial of some value as a companion plant or in wetter wildflower meadows where it can spread readily. Historically a useful herb in brewing and dyeing, but can be highly toxic if taken internally or externally.

H: 24–36 in (60–90 cm); **S**: 18 in (45 cm) ✲✲✲ ◌ ☼

Taraxacum officinale
The dandelion is not a herb that is likely to be deliberately cultivated as it can become a problem weed if allowed to set seed. However, the young leaves are a tasty addition to salads and the dried root makes a caffeine-free alternative to coffee.

H: 3 in (8 cm); **S**: 6 in (15 cm)
✲✲✲ ◌ ☼

Teucrium chamaedrys
This herb forms a mat of evergreen foliage with upright flowers. Easily grown as a low hedge in a sunny, well-drained soil, it also thrives in walls and rockeries. Propagate by division in spring and keep in shape by clipping in spring and fall.

H: 12 in (30 cm); **S**: 12 in (30 cm)
✲✲✲ ◌ ☼

Teucrium x lucidrys
A hybrid germander with aromatic, slightly spicy-scented glossy leaves, it is a good ground cover plant for a sunny, well-drained position and is often used in herb parterres. Easy to propagate by division in spring or by semi-hardwood cuttings in summer.

H: 12–20 in (30–50 cm); **S**: 12 in (30 cm) ✲✲✲ ◌ ☼

Thymus citriodorus

This is an excellent culinary thyme with larger lemon-scented, hairless, green leaves and pale pink flowers. It forms a bushy, rounded mound if kept well trimmed. The trimmings can then be dried or frozen in ice cubes for future use.

H: 12 in (30 cm); **S**: 10 in (25 cm)
❆ ❆ ❆ ◊ ☼

Thymus **Coccineus Group**

Matt-forming with trailing stems covered in finely haired small leaves. Its attractive, crimson-pink flowers are attractive to bees. Deadheading can be tricky and is more easily done using kitchen scissors. Propagate from cuttings in late summer.

H: 10 in (25 cm); **S**: 18 in (45 cm)
❆ ❆ ❆ ◊ ☼

Thymus doerfleri "Bressingham"

This thyme is a compact spreading sub-shrub with low-lying hairy stems. The aromatic gray-green leaves contrast with the clear pink flowers in summer. Plant the thyme in well-drained soil and remove any leaves that fall onto it in fall.

H: 4 in (10 cm); **S**: 14 in (35 cm)
❆ ❆ ❆ ◊ ☼

Thymus "Fragrantissimus"

The leaves of this compact bushy thyme are small and grayish-green with a lovely spicey orange scent. Deadhead or trim regularly to keep in shape and collect the cuttings for use in the kitchen. It is easy to propagate from seeds or cuttings.

H: 12 in (30 cm); **S**: 8 in (20 cm)
❆ ❆ ❆ ◊ ☼

Thymus "Golden King"

Strongly lemon scented with gold-margined, mid-green leaves. This variety is slightly more upright than its cousins if kept well trimmed and is easy to grow as a culinary herb in a container or windowbox in a bright sunny situation.

H: 10 in (25 cm); **S**: 18 in (45 cm)
❆ ❆ ❆ ◊ ☼

Thymus officinalis

The essential ingredient of bouquet garnis, with its aromatic, slightly hairy leaves, this is the traditional culinary and medicinal thyme. The mauve flowers are very attractive to bees and it is easy to grow from seed if surface sown in early spring.

H: 10 in (25 cm); **S**: 18 in (45 cm)
❆ ❆ ❆ ◊ ☼

Plant guide (Th–Zi)

Thymus praecox
This herb is a lovely small, creeping thyme that cross-pollinates and hybridizes readily. Many named cultivars can be unreliably scented, but some have a delightful orange or nutmeg scent. For consistency, only propagate from cuttings.

H: 2 in (5 cm); **S**: 24 in (60 cm)
❄❄❄ ◊ ☼

Thymus pulegioides "Bertram Anderson"
A very decorative thyme with a mild thyme scent. It forms a rounded mound and is more substantially gold colored than many cultivars. Like all thymes, it dislikes being tread upon, but is useful between pavers.

H: 12 in (30 cm); **S**: 10 in (25 cm)
❄❄❄ ◊ ☼

Thymus serpyllum
Forms a dense mat that needs trimming regularly in summer to promote new growth and to prevent the mound spreading open. Many cultivars exist, which should be propagated from cuttings as seed will not produce true to type progeny.

H: 10 in (25 cm); **S**: 18 in (45 cm)
❄❄❄ ◊ ☼

Thymus serpyllum "Minimalist"
A very low-growing thyme with tiny leaves and pink flowers. Forms a compact mat rapidly if grown in a sunny, sharply-drained site. To prevent die-back and rotting, remove all fallen leaves and other detritus throughout the year.

H: 2 in (5 cm); **S**: 4 in (10 cm)
❄❄❄ ◊ ☼

Thymus vulgaris "Erectus"
Upright thyme is an unusual form of common thyme, as instead of spreading, the stems grow upward, resembling a small conifer. It grows slowly and the narrow leaves are packed with white flowers appearing in summer that attract bees.

H: 6–12 in (15–30 cm); **S**: 16 in (40 cm) ❄❄❄ ◊ ☼

Thymus vulgaris "Siver Posie"
A lovely evergreen thyme with silver and gray variegations. It is quite vigorous, so needs regular trimming to keep in shape. Young plants can be cut back by half immediately after flowering—retain some trimmings as cutting material.

H: 6–12 in (15–30 cm); **S**: 16 in (40 cm) ❄❄❄ ◊ ☼

Tropaeolum majus **Alaska Series**

A very easy-to-grow annual for sunny and shady positions. The leaves and flowers of nasturtiums are edible and both look and taste good in salads. Collect the large caperlike seeds in late summer and store in a cool, dry place for sowing the following spring.

H: 3–10 ft (1–3 mm); **S**: 5–15 ft (1.5–5 m) ❋◊ ◐ ☼ ♔

Valeriana officinalis

This tall, very variable plant is easy to grow in any damp, shady spot and is ideal in a wildflower meadow. It is valued medicinally as a sedative, but is addictive and has other adverse side effects. Sow seed in spring or divide clumps in the fall.

H: 4–6 ft (1.2–2 m); **S**: 16–32 in (40–80 cm) ❋❋❋ ◊ ◐ ☼ ☀

Verbena officinalis

Used in homoeopathy for a variety of disorders, such as insomnia and migraines, and once believed to ward off plague, only use *Verbena officinalis* under medical supervision. It self-seeds readily and is best grown in the wildflower meadow.

H: 24 in (60 cm); **S**: 20 in (50 cm) ❋❋❋ ◊ ◐ ☼

Viola odorata

This sweet-smelling hardy perennial herb is widely used in perfumery and medicinal remedies, such as a diuretic tea that alleviates rheumatic pain. The colorful leaves can be added to salads and the flowers are often candied or used as a garnish.

H: 8 in (20 cm); **S**: 12 in (30 cm) ❋❋❋ ◊ ◐ ☼ ☀

Viola tricolor

An easy-to-grow, short-lived perennial, heartsease is best grown as an annual from seed, sown in the ground in spring. The leaves and flowers are edible, but in excess may cause vomiting. Deadhead regularly to promote new flower growth.

H: 3–5 in (8–12 cm); **S**: 4–6 in (10–15 cm) ❋❋❋ ◊ ◐ ☼ ☀

Zingiber officinale

Fresh ginger can be grown, but high temperatures are essential, so this is one best planted indoors. Plant a firm, plump sprouting root just below the surface of a well-drained compost in a conservatory or greenhouse at a minimum 68°F (20°C).

H: 4 ft (1.2 m); **S**: 24 in (60 cm) ❀◊ ☼

Suppliers

Many of these suppliers are specialized nurseries, so it is worth checking for opening hours before visiting, especially if you are making a long trip.

Backyard Gardener
PO Box 23598
Federal Way
WA 98093-0598
www.backyardgardener.com

Barn Owl Nursery
22999 SW Newland Road
Wilsonville
OR 97070
Tel: 503-638-0387

Blossom Farm
34515 Capel Road
Columbia Station
OH 44028
Tel: 330-529-5737 (voice mail)
www.blossomfarm.com

Blue Heron Herbary
27731 NW Reeder Road
Sauvies Island
OR 97231
Tel: 503-621-1457
www.blueheronherbary.com

Cate Farm
135 Cate Farm Rd
Plainfield
VT 05667
Tel: 802-454-7157
www.catefarm.com

Crimson Sage Nursery
PO Box 83
Orleans
CA 95556
Tel: 530-627-3457
www.crimson-sage.com

Dry Creek Herb Farm
13935 Dry Creek Road
Auburn
CA 95602
Tel: 530-268-3638
www.drycreekherbfarm.com

Gaia Herbs
108 Island Ford Road
Brevard
NC 28712
Tel: 800-831-7780
www.gaiaherbs.com

Good Earth Gardens
3311 Ann Arbor Drive
Houston
TX 77063
Tel: 936-588-794
www.goodearthliveherbs.com

HerbFresh.com
Tel: 760-451-1183
www.herbfresh.com

J.W. Jung Seed Company
335 South High Street
Randolph
WI 53956
Tel: 800-297-3123
www.jungseed.com

Lingle's Herbs
2055 North Lomina Avenue
Long Beach
CA 90815
Tel: 562-598-4372
www.linglesherbs.com

Medicinal Herb Plants & Crimson Sage Nursery
PO Box 83
Orleans
CA 95556
Tel: 530-627-3457
www.medicinalherbplants.com

Morningsun Herb Farm
6137 Pleasants Valley Road
Vacaville
CA 95688
Tel: 707-451-9406
www.morningsunherbfarm.com

Mountain Valley Growers
38325 Pepperweed Road
Squaw Valley
CA 93675
Tel: 559-338-2775
www.mountainvalleygrowers.com

Mulberry Creek Herb Farm
3312 Bogart Road
Huron
OH 44839
Tel: 419-433-6126
www.mulberrycreek.com

Papa Geno's Herb Farm
6005 West Roca Road
Martell
NE 68404
Tel: 402-794-0400
www.papagenos.com

Paula's Herbs and Plants
PO Box 185
Omega
GA 31775
paulasherbsandplants.com

Possum Creek Herb Farm
528 Nature Trail
Soddy Daisy
TN 37379
Tel: 423-718-3533
possumcreekherb.com

Sand Mountain Herbs
Hway 75
Fyffe
AL 35962
www.sandmountainherbs.com

Sandy Mush Herb Nursery
316 Surrett Cove Road
Leicester
North Carolina 28748
Tel: 828-683-2014
www.sandymushherbs.com

The Thyme Garden Herb Company
20546 Alsea Highway
Alsea
OR 97324
Tel: 541-487-8671
www.thymegarden.com

White Flower Farm
PO Box 50
Route 63
Litchfield
Connecticut 06759
Tel: 888-466-8849
www.whiteflowerfarm.com

Zack Woods Herb Farm
278 Mead Rd
Hyde Park
VT 05655
Tel: 802-888-7278
www.zackwoodsherbs.com/

Herb Research Foundation
4140 15th Street
Boulder
CO 80304
Tel: 303-449-2265
www.herbs.org

The Herb Society of America
9010 Kirtland Chardon Road
Kirtland
OH 44094
Tel: 440-256-0514
www.ahaherb.com

Other useful addresses

American Botanical Council
PO Box 144345
Austin
TX 78714-4345
Tel: 512-926-4900
abc.herbalgram.org

The American Herb Association
PO Box 1673
Nevada City
CA 95959
Tel: 530-265-9552
www.ahaherb.com

The Herb Growing & Marketing Network
PO Box 245
Silver Spring
PA 17575-0245
Tel: 717-393-3295
www.herbnet.com

Index

Index

Acknowledgments

The publisher would like to thank the following for their kind permission to reproduce their photographs:

(Key: a-above; b-below/bottom; c-center; l-left; r-right; t-top)

2: Elizabeth Whiting & Associates/www. ewastock.com. **6–7:** Elizabeth Whiting & Associates/www.ewastock.com. **10:** The Garden Collection: Derek St Romaine: Design: Cleve West (t), Derek Harris (br), Clive Nichols: Design: Hedens Lustgard, Sweden (bl). **11:** Clive Nichols: Hunmanby Grange, Yorkshire. **12:** GAP Photos: Elke Borkowski (t), The Garden Collection: Nicola Stocken Tomkins (b). **13:** The Garden Collection: Torie Chugg/Design: Andy Kirman, RHS Tatton Park 2006 (t), Photolibrary: Howard Rice (b). **14:** The Garden Collection: Andrew Lawson/ Helmingham Hall, Suffolk. **15:** The Garden Collection: Nicola Stocken Tomkins (t), Liz Eddison/Design: Jane Peterson (br); Clive Nichols: RHS Chelsea 2008, Daylesford Organic (bl). **17:** GAP Photos: Clive Nichols (tr); Leigh Clapp (tl). **66:** Simon Charlesworth/www.downderry-nursery. co.uk (cl). **67:** Clive Nichols: Design: Nuala Hancock & Mathew Bell,Chelsea Flower Show 1994. **68:** Simon Charlesworth/ www.downderry-nursery.co.uk: (tl). **69:** The Garden Collection: Derek Harris. **70–71:** The Garden Collection: Jonathan Buckley/ Design Tommaso del Buono & Paul Gazerwitz, RHS Chelsea Flower Show 2008 (t). **75:** The Garden Collection: LIz Eddison. **76–77:** The Garden Collection: Derek St Romaine/Mr & Mrs Jolley, Maycotts, Kent (t). **79:** Photolibrary: J S Sira,: Design: Michael Miller, RHS Chelsea 2001. **81:** The Garden Collection: Liz Eddison/Design: Jeff Groundrill, RHS Chelsea Flower Show 2001. **85:** GAP Photos: Ron Evans. **86–87:** Photolibrary: Linda Burgess (t). **88–89:** The Garden Collection: Liz Eddison/Design: Gillian McCulloch, RHS Tatton Park 2007 (t). **103:** DK Images: Malcolm Coulson (br). **110:** David Murphy: (tr). **120:** Simon Charlesworth/www.downderry-nursery. co.uk: (tc). **121:** Simon Charlesworth/ www.downderry-nursery.co.uk: (tc) (br) (bl)

All other images © Dorling Kindersley

For further information see: www.dkimages.com